EFFECTIVE LEADERSHIP

in early childhood and primary
school education in Aotearoa New Zealand

EFFECTIVE LEADERSHIP

in early childhood and primary
school education in Aotearoa New Zealand

Edited by Tracey Carlyon and Rosina Merry

NZCER PRESS
Te Pakokori
Level 4, 10 Brandon St,
Wellington

www.nzcer.org.nz

© Authors, 2024

ISBN 978-1-99-004096-2

No part of the publication may be copied, stored, or communicated in any form by any means (paper or digital), including recording or storing in an electronic retrieval system, without the written permission of the publisher.
Education institutions that hold a current licence with Copyright Licensing New Zealand may copy from this book in strict accordance with the terms of the CLNZ Licence.

A catalogue record for this book is available from the National Library of New Zealand.

Designed by Smartwork Creative

Foreword

Arguably the most important catalyst for change and improvement in education settings is educational leadership. This book, *Effective Leadership in Early Childhood Services and Primary School Education in Aotearoa New Zealand*, promotes educational leadership as being important and that it "matters" (Harris & Jones, 2023). It is designed to examine, comment on, critique, and reflect upon the nuanced activities of educational leadership. In utilising their experiences and expertise as educators, educational leaders, and researchers from both sectors to explore effective educational leadership, the authors emphasise the importance of effective leadership. They do not write about the mechanics of leadership, rather they endeavour, albeit in different ways, to speak directly to readers who want to know more about educational leadership and the elements that contribute to its effectiveness.

Three distinct parts offer readers guidance to navigate the book's 12 chapters. Part 1 explores concepts and practices of leadership through cultural and contextual lenses. Parts 2 and 3 focus respectively on the early childhood and primary school sectors. The themes of relationships, relational leadership, bicultural leadership, Pacific leadership, change and transition, emotion in the context of change, cross-sector collaboration, middle leadership, wellbeing, systems convening ways of leading, and professional learning are presented as crucial themes for consideration and reflection in the primary and early childhood education sectors.

This book is by no means intended to be "how to do leadership", rather it seeks to contribute to current and diverse leadership conversations among primary and early childhood educators in Aotearoa New Zealand by drawing on a variety of leadership concepts and contexts. Those leading in early childhood services and primary school education accept there is no magic to conjure up a seamless integration of political, economic, ideological, theoretical, and philosophical principles to create the perfect climate for enacting effective educational leadership. Hence, the importance of generating ongoing dialogue about effective educational leadership. Through their exploration of educational leadership in a variety of contexts, the book's authors continue to highlight themes that retain urgency. While these will be familiar to readers, in the book they are examined in contemporary contexts. Notably, some authors have drawn upon their own research; thus, adding to readers' understanding of topics that have been potentially less researched and/or under-researched.

Not only does this book have the potential to liberate leaders by motivating them to expand their knowledge and understanding, but it encourages commitment to extending their thinking about effective leadership and range of practices. In exploring concepts, examining research and the literature, conducting research, and inquiring into best practices in various contexts and through diverse lenses, this book emphasises the vital nature of effective educational leadership for primary school and early childhood services improvement. The book will likely affirm and provoke thinking, reflection, action-taking, study, and further research. It will certainly be of service to those seeking to develop and improve leadership—their own and in collaboration with others.

Dr Jenny Ferrier-Kerr
Educator

September 2024

Reference

Harris, A., & Jones, M. (2023). The importance of school leadership? What we know. *School Leadership & Management, 43*(5), 449–453. https://doi.org/10.1080/13632434.2023.2287806

Preface

Welcome to *Effective Leadership in Early Childhood Services and Primary School Education in Aotearoa New Zealand*. This pukapuka presents a collection of chapters each focused on effective leadership within a specific context or sector. The chapters are authored by academic staff members at Te Rito Maioha (ECNZ), who bring experience and expertise to their respective chapter topics. The authors are practitioners who are committed to enacting effective leadership in their own practice, in addition to supporting others to do so. The pukapuka is intended for early childhood educators and primary school teachers and leaders: however, it will be useful for teachers and leaders from the secondary sector, initial teacher education and vocational education training providers, and policymakers.

For the cover we have chosen a huia feather in acknowledgement of Te Rito Maioha's bicultural kaupapa. In Māori culture, the huia feather is a cherished symbol of leadership, respect, and mana. These feathers were worn by both men and women in their hair or around their necks. Although the huia is now extinct, its significance remains alive in te ao Māori and is reflected in various whakataukī including "Huia e huia, tangata kotahi," meaning "Huia, your destiny is to bring people together." As such, the huia feather serves as a fitting symbol of the effective leadership showcased throughout the chapters of this pukapuka.

The pukapuka comprises three parts. Part 1 gives attention to leadership within cultures and contexts. Parts 2 and 3 focus on leadership within the early childhood and primary school sectors respectively. Several chapters are informed by practical experience or originate from specific topics that are of particular interest to the authors. Other chapters derive from empirical research directly relating to leadership, including individual staff members' master's and/or doctoral studies. The pukapuka is greater than the sum of its parts, with the chapter authors all bringing extensive knowledge and expertise to build a rich understanding of effective leadership.

While each of the 12 chapters are independent of each other, the synergies between them are clear. First, it is evident that effective leadership within education is critical, regardless of context or sector. Second, there are several key characteristics and behaviours that emerge which effective leaders consistently demonstrate in their practice. Some of the characteristics effective leaders demonstrate include being relational, supportive, trustworthy, authentic, caring, empowering, and adaptable. In addition, effective leaders are shown to be good communicators, who prioritise wellbeing and have the skills to develop a culture that is supportive of risk-taking and inclusive of a common vision. Even though this list of characteristics and behaviours is not exhaustive, collectively it provides a platform for aspiring leaders, and those already in leadership positions, from which to reflect, discuss, and take action to improve leadership within different contexts and sectors.

We began this pukapuka to support those teachers and leaders working within education settings in Aotearoa New Zealand. With a particular focus on early childhood services and the primary sector, the inclusion of chapters based on varied topics and contexts was deliberate in order to provide readers with a broad view of effective leadership. The pukapuka opens up a raft of theoretical and practical ideas for educational leaders to reflect on. In addition, it will perhaps encourage them to undertake research to generate further practice-based evidence that contributes to the body of educational leadership knowledge.

Dr Tracey Carlyon and Dr Rosina Merry
Editors

Contents

Foreword v

Preface vii

PART 1

LEADERSHIP WITHIN CULTURES AND CONTEXTS 1

Chapter 1 Walking backwards into the future (Ka mua, ka muri): Insights on Māori education leadership for primary and early childhood leaders 3
Tui Summers and Sandra Tuhakaraina
Introduction 3
The historical context of Māori leadership 4
A framework for Māori leadership 8
Conclusion 15
Glossary of te reo Māori terms 18

Chapter 2 The distinct nature of Pacific leadership: Applying this within early childhood education and primary schools in Aotearoa New Zealand 20
Anoop Kumar
Introduction 20
History of Pacific leadership 20
Representation of Pacific people in leadership roles within Aotearoa New Zealand 21
The way forward 28
Conclusion 29

Chapter 3 Systems-convening leadership and cross-sector collaboration 32
Tiffany Williams
Introduction 32
The study 34
Communicating a clear vision for improvement 35
Building a collaborative culture built on relational trust 36
Sharing of diverse teacher expertise 38
Conclusion 40

Chapter 4 Navigating emotional responses to educational change: Empowering leaders through knowledge and action 43
Beth Germaine
Introduction 43
Emotional responses to change in educational settings 44
A framework for navigating emotional responses to change 49
Conclusion 55

PART 2

LEADERSHIP WITHIN THE EARLY CHILDHOOD SECTOR   59

Chapter 5 Exploring notions of early childhood leadership in Aotearoa New Zealand   61
Gwen Davitt and Debbie Ryder
Introduction   61
Realities of ECE leadership   62
Changing perception of ECE leadership   63
A dispositional approach for ECE leadership   64
Conclusion   69

Chapter 6 Experiences of leading an early childhood education centre during the COVID-19 pandemic   72
Jo Ellis and Rachel Taylor
Introduction   72
Impact on leaders' wellbeing   74
Challenges of leading during COVID-19   75
Strategies to effectively lead an ECE centre through COVID-19   78
Conclusion   82

Chapter 7 Professional learning to support effective leadership in early childhood education   85
Penny Smith and Monica Cameron
Introduction   85
The study   87
Findings: Critical aspects of effective leadership   88
Impact of engaging in the programme   91
Opportunities for implementing leadership   95
Conclusion   96

Chapter 8 Growing associate teachers' capacity to be leaders: Recognising effective leadership during practicum   99
Debbie Woolston and Claire Wilson
Introduction   99
Relationships   101
Communication   102
Mentoring   103
Ako   105
Vulnerability   106
Conclusion   108

PART 3

LEADERSHIP WITHIN THE PRIMARY SCHOOL SECTOR — 113

Chapter 9 Leading primary schools in Aotearoa New Zealand: The role and challenges of school leaders — 115
J Clark McPhillips and Tracey Carlyon

Introduction — 115
The study — 117
How school leaders see their role — 118
The challenges school leaders currently face — 123
Conclusion — 128

Chapter 10 Successful teacher change and transition: The role of primary school leaders — 132
Tracey Carlyon

Introduction — 132
The study — 133
The role of school leaders — 134
Relational trust — 135
Support — 136
Collaboration — 138
Common vision — 139
Conclusion — 140

Chapter 11 Middle leadership in primary schools in Aotearoa New Zealand — 145
Richard Edwards

Introduction — 145
Middle leadership in education — 146
What do middle leaders do? — 148
Who is the middle leader? — 150
Vignette of a middle leader — 151
Conclusion — 154

Chapter 12 Relational leadership: Teachers' perceptions of leaders' behaviours and actions — 158
Anthony Fisher

Introduction — 158
The study — 159
Relational leadership styles — 160
Teachers' perspectives on building relationships with their principals — 162
Conclusion — 167

INDEX — 170

ABOUT THE AUTHORS — 176

PART 1

LEADERSHIP WITHIN CULTURES AND CONTEXTS

Chapter 1

Walking backwards into the future (Ka mua, ka muri): Insights on Māori education leadership for primary and early childhood leaders

Tui Summers and Sandra Tuhakaraina

Introduction

Whiria matua kaha ngā uara o te rauhuia, hei tohu o haututanga. Bind tightly the values of huia feather as a symbol of leadership.

This chapter[1] focuses on the unique and special nature of leadership from a Māori perspective in the early childhood and primary education sectors in Aotearoa New Zealand. The chapter answers the questions: What does historical and contemporary literature tell us about the history of Māori leadership and what can we learn from this? What does Māori leadership look like in the early childhood and primary education sectors?

The chapter is organised in two sections. The first section gives an overview of the historical context for Māori leadership. The second section gives a framework, developed by the authors of this chapter, based on literature and research about Māori leadership. The framework outlines some principles of Māori leadership and an overview of

---

1   It is expected readers will be familiar with many of the te reo Māori terms used in this chapter. A glossary is provided at the end of the chapter and in-text translations are provided for lesser-known terms to aid clarity.

how these principles can be applied in early childhood education and primary education leadership and practice.

The intent of this chapter is to provide a broader context of Māori leadership for education leaders whether they are in early childhood or primary settings and whether they are in a teaching role or a designated leadership position. This chapter also intends to equip leaders in early childhood and primary settings with some definitions of what Māori leadership comprises and what it looks like in practice.

The historical context of Māori leadership

Kōrero tuku iho—A period of harmony

He aha te kai ō te rangatira? He kōrero, he kōrero. What is the food of the leader? It is knowledge. It is communication.

Historically, Māori leadership existed in the fabric of the landscape of Aotearoa New Zealand. The social structures of Māori society included marae, iwi, hapū, and whānau. The cultural values of manaakitanga, whanaungatanga, and whakapapa were embedded and were practised within these structures (Summers, 2022). Early tūpuna navigated from Hawaiki, Pacific Islands to Aotearoa and returned to Hawaiki to tell of these explorations. Under leadership guidance of tohunga, ariki, and rangatira, waka voyages commenced. These expeditions were carefully organised and structured by earlier tūpuna (Katene, 2010; Spiller et al., 2015). Māori ancestral heroes such as Kupe and Māui showed leadership qualities of resilience, risk-taking, strategy, and bravery (Walker, 2004). As a result, leadership flourished on marae, with iwi, hapū, and whānau through kaumātua, tohunga, ariki, and rangatira (Katene, 2013).

The whakapapa of Māori leadership is essential to understanding leadership in the Māori world. In examining Māori leadership, it is evident that this leadership evolved within te ao Māori, a distinctive cultural worldview, deep-rooted in the values and beliefs of ancestors of Aotearoa New Zealand. A central facet of te ao Māori is the Māori creation story which encompasses cosmology including Ranginui (sky father), Papatūānuku (mother earth), and their tamariki. Iwi had autonomy over their lives; iwi were born into and lived in a universe that was entirely a Māori way of knowing, being, and doing (Katene, 2013; Smith, 2012).

Te reo Māori was a mode of oral communication and a living language that thrived within all iwi, hapū, and whānau communities. Te reo Māori practices of saying your whakapapa—"Ko wai au?" (Who am I?), "Nō hea koe?" (Where do I belong?)—included genealogy links back to waka and the cosmos. Whakataukī were naturally woven into the living language. Waiata were sung for all occasions and events to retain the whakapapa for the people (Hemara, 2000).

Traditionally, two types of leaders were recognised in Māori society (Katene, 2010). These were rangatira and tohunga (Walker, 2004). These roles could be ascribed or inherited, and their leadership covered the spiritual, professional, or political arenas (Durie, 1998). Historically, an example of a rangatira was a chief specialising in political leadership (Ballara, 1998). Katene (2010) explains that "in the traditional setting a rangatira could be male or female" (p. 4). An ariki could also be a man or a woman (Katene, 2010). For example, Dame Atairangikaahu from the Kīngitanga was a notable female ariki who served many in her iwi (Walker, 2004). The second type of leader, tohunga, was seen to have special qualities and prowess related to spirituality, religion, and areas such as agriculture and conservation (Katene, 2010). Although these two leadership types are represented independently here, traditionally Māori leaders had overlapping roles and responsibilities. For example, an ariki could also be a tohunga.

Growing traditional leadership was undertaken by leaders of iwi, hapū, and marae. Iwi leaders would observe, recognise, and select future leaders, who were ascribed leadership or it as a birthright (Ka'ai & Reilly, 2012). Wānanga (places of learning) were saturated in traditional ways of knowing, being, and doing by the collective leaders on behalf of the iwi, hapū, and whānau. These leaders of expertise imparted sacred knowledge through intergenerational learning in the same fashion that had been handed down by their ancestors and leaders.

Kōrero tuku iho—A time of broken harmony

He kai kei aku ringa. There is food at the end of my hands. This whakataukī illustrates a leader's authority to create success or disrupt communities.

Leadership stability, strength, and solidarity amongst iwi, hapū, and whānau started to unravel. This period is a time of broken harmony as new groups such as whalers, traders, sealers, missionaries, and settlers came to Aotearoa. These new groups brought new technologies, and new values—both tangible and intangible—that benefited, but mostly interrupted and changed, a way of being in well-established Māori communities.

Following the first colonial encounters between Māori and British settlers, Whakaputanga o te Rangatiratanga o Nu Tireni (Declaration of the Independence of New Zealand) and Te Tiriti o Waitangi (Treaty of Waitangi), became the founding documents of Aotearoa (Hayward, 2004; Riwai-Couch, 2022). The latter was signed by rangatira Māori and representatives of the British Crown, with aspirations to bring unity, collaboration, law, and peace. However, for Māori, the effects of the colonial encounter weakened Māori leadership practices, moving from a well-established and organised collective system to prioritising individual needs of education (Ka'ai & Reilly, 2012). The onslaught of colonisation, assimilation, and urbanisation ruptured the foundation of Māori social structures.

Jenkins and Morris Matthews (2005) note early wāhine Māori teaching in Mission schools were leaders of their time, well versed in the Māori language and tikanga Māori. They taught using Māori language and cultural values alongside the Native Schools Act. The whakapapa of Māori knowledge was excluded following the introduction of the Education Act 1867, which stipulated that curriculum learning and instructions be conducted in the English language. One of the detrimental effects of the legislation was the exclusion and erosion of Māori language, culture, and identity for te reo Māori speakers.

Kōrero tuku iho—*A rebuilding of harmony*

E kore au e ngaro, he kākano i ruia mai i Rangiātea. I will never be lost, for I am a seed sown in Rangiātea.

Māori leaders and community voices joined collectively in the 1970s to protest, advocate, and assert mana motuhake (self-determination) to reclaim Māori rights to language, culture, and identity as guaranteed in both early historical documents. This can be likened to the karanga, a ceremonial call fulfilled by kaikaranga, who weave individuals into the collective realm of the living and non-living. Māori looked back at the past, for answers within, to overcome the demise in education places to create a more hopeful future. The answers came from within the collective people, and from a traditional strategy of kotahitanga (unity and oneness).

What followed from the collective voices was a resurgence of kaupapa Māori education environments as a form of resistance to disrupt decades of the dominance of Western knowledge, values, and practice and the erasure of Māori knowledge, values, and beliefs.

Research on Māori leadership in both traditional and contemporary Māori society has emphasised the importance of kaumātua and kuia and has found how most Māori leadership occurs within iwi, hapū, and on the marae (Tapiata et al., 2020; Te Momo, 2011). Kaumātua and kuia play an important part in growing leadership and role-modelling qualities they want to be reflected in tamariki and mokopuna, who are the future generations (Jahnke, 1997).

An example of leadership in te ao Māori is the esteemed kaumātua and kuia that led the Te Māori exhibition across museums in the USA in 1986 (Durie, 2021). Te Māori was the first major international art exhibition where Indigenous taonga from Aotearoa were collected and showcased to an international audience (Mead, 1986). Māori accompanied the exhibition in various capacities, including as kaitiaki, performers, officials, and weavers (Department of Māori Affairs Te Māori Management Committee, 1988). These decades of research have shown that the identification of kaumātua and kuia is pivotal to Māori leadership.

Te Kōhanga Reo is recognised nationally and internationally as a successful movement, although tensions do exist. Te Kōhanga Reo was set up by kaumātua and leaders to restore whānau empowerment, whānau participation, and the revitalisation of te reo me ōna tikanga Māori. Tuhakaraina and Dayman (2020) describe kaumātua as "the glue" (p. 93) who were influential in the revitalising, decolonising, and transforming the lives of non reo Māori speaking parents, tamariki, and whānau who did not completely understand the full impact of colonisation and assimilation. The success of Te Kōhanga Reo can be seen in contemporary times in the employment of confident and competent Māori, strong in their sense of language, culture, and identity, in education, law, media, politics, and so forth.

After over 40 years of Te Kōhanga Reo, combined with other initiatives such as kura kaupapa Māori (Māori immersion schooling), evidence in education spaces of the Māori language, culture, and identity is growing. Tamariki who attended kura kaupapa Māori or bilingual education developed a deep sense of identity and deep knowledge of te ao Māori and wellbeing.

A framework for Māori leadership

Nāu te rourou, nāku te rourou, ka ora ai te iwi. With your basket and my basket, the people will thrive.

This section provides a framework developed by the authors for what Māori leadership is, based on contemporary literature and research. The framework outlines how Māori leadership can be applied in early childhood education and primary education leadership and practice.

A pivotal factor in Māori leadership is being able to demonstrate a Te Tiriti o Waitangi bicultural partnership. Leaders must be willing to engage, lead, and support teaching teams to intentionally plan and design a curriculum that embraces reciprocal and respectful relationships with partners of Te Tiriti. Seven mātauranga Māori principles identified by the authors as being commonly cited in the Māori educational leadership literature as critical features of reclamation of Māori leadership qualities in early childhood and school leadership practice are presented here. These are: whakapapa (identity); whanaungatanga (relationships, connections); manaakitanga (hospitality); te reo me ngā tikanga (Māori language and protocols); aroha (love); mauri ora (life force); and tangata whenuatanga (place-based ways of being, doing, and knowing).

When considering these principles, there are three points that are important to consider. Firstly, te ao Māori is a collective as opposed to an individual culture, and these principles need to be considered in this context. For example, on the marae, whānau members work collaboratively to achieve common goals such as hosting manuhiri (guests) for important hui. Secondly, there is significant variation across whānau, hapū, and iwi in relation to te reo me ngā tikanga Māori, whakapapa, and pūrākau (storytelling). Māori are not a homogeneous group, and respect needs to be practised to reflect that these differences exist. Thirdly, these principles are presented independent of each other; however, they do overlap and should be used in a holistic way to reflect te ao Māori and the interdependent nature of the early childhood curriculum, *Te Whāriki: He Whāriki Mātauranga mō ngā Mokopuna o Aotearoa* (Ministry of Education, 1996, 2017) and the primary school curriculum, *The New Zealand Curriculum: For English-medium Teaching and Learning in Years 1–13* (Ministry of Education, 2007).

Whakapapa

Whakapapa is lineage, kinship, and family connections. In order to enact Māori leadership from the tikanga principle, leaders need to know themselves and instil in others the importance of knowing themselves by addressing the questions: "Ko wai au?" (Who am I?) and "Nō hea au?" (Where do I belong?). Whakapapa knowledge of the local iwi, hapū, and marae is important. Leadership in relation to whakapapa may mean supporting Māori to learn the whakapapa connection between themselves and their marae. Similarly, knowing where and how to find iwi of your community reflects a commitment to and prioritisation of te ao Māori. Whakapapa is also about the landscape (Kelly & Nicholson, 2021). Knowing the deep-rooted narratives of the land, mountains, rivers, and oceans and retelling them through waiata, whakataukī, pepeha, and pūrākau enriches learning experiences.

Critical awareness of whakapapa knowledge as a leader enhances the mana of those around the leader.

Whanaungatanga

Whanaungatanga is about relationships and connections. Enacting Māori leadership from the tikanga principle of whanaungatanga is supporting respectful and authentic relationships with colleagues, parents, whānau, and the wider community that is inclusive of kaumātua, iwi, and hapū. Ongoing connections and communication through face-to-face and other forms of dialogue is essential if whanaungatanga is going to flourish in education spaces. Inclusion of whānau is at the heart of whanaungatanga. The promotion of ako (teaching and learning) relationships, where teaching and learning are reciprocal, must be encouraged and supported. Critical awareness of whanaungatanga is the leader's connection to the learner's identity, language, and culture.

Manaakitanga

Manaakitanga is hospitality, taking care of people, and being careful about how people are treated (Mead, 2016). This view is supported further by Williams and Broadley (2012), who explain manaakitanga as derived from two principal words: "mana" meaning prestige, status, reputation, self-esteem; and "aki", the shortened version of akiaki, meaning to uplift, build upon, strengthen. Therefore, manaakitanga involves the complex act of ensuring one's personal mana remains intact by protecting the mana of others. An example of manaakitanga on the marae is the role of tangata whenua (hosts), where they welcome and show hospitality to manuhiri. The experience of the visitors reflects on the mana of the tangata whenua. Sharing in kai is considered practising manaakitanga. Manaakitanga leadership begins with your mana and how you engage, empower, and treat others. A leader who practises manaakitanga is observant and recognises the potential in others to uplift and strengthen their mana.

Te reo me ngā tikanga

Te reo Māori is one of three official languages of Aotearoa.[2] According to the Ministry of Education (2013), high-quality Māori language in education "supports identity, language and culture as critical, but not exclusive, ingredients for the success of all Māori students" (p. 28). Moreover, te reo me ngā tikanga "supports community and iwi commitments to Māori language intergenerational transmission and language survival" (p. 28). Ability in te reo me ngā tikanga is crucial for leaders to understand, actively use, and engage learners through daily use of practices such as waiata, whakataukī, pūrākau, and karakia. The Māori language is still in a critical state of survival, but it is envisaged that working collectively and collaboratively as a team will positively change this state.

Aroha

Aroha is closely related to whanaungatanga. Aroha is often translated to mean love. However, it is more complex and includes the concepts of love, charity, and sympathy (Love, 2004; Pere, 1997). At the heart of aroha is a range of te ao Māori concepts for leaders and kaiako to nurture amongst colleagues, when interacting with whānau and with tamariki. Examples of these concepts include whakapono (belief, trust), wairua (spirituality), manaaki, and whakakoakoa (happiness, joy) (Ministry of Education, 2017).

Mauri ora

Mauri is the lifeforce of all living and non-living things and flows through all things—land, trees, rivers, mountains, space, and time, through to people—individually and collectively. Pohatu and Pohatu (2011) express mauri as the formation of human relationships. Mauri therefore highlights the "how and why" we shape how we learn, lead, and behave (p. 1). Ora is wellness. Mauri ora is the notion of Māori living and succeeding as Māori. The way mauri ora is expressed by leaders can impact on other people; in fact, the mauri ora of each person can impact on others such as whānau members, colleagues, and tamariki.

---

2   Te reo Māori and New Zealand Sign Language are official languages by legislation, English is considered a de facto official language due to widespread use.

Tangata whenuatanga

This principle is about affirming Māori and their cultural background and context. Tangata whenuatanga is a modern term and is one of five cultural competencies listed in the document *Tātaiako: Cultural Competencies for Teachers of Māori Learners* (Education Council New Zealand, 2011). The competency aims to develop place-based, sociocultural awareness and knowledge for designing local curriculum about the environment, the local marae, hapū, and whānau (Education Council New Zealand, 2011). An example of tangata whenuatanga is when iwi pūrākau are known and encouraged in the curriculum by leaders.

These seven principles are presented in Table 1.1, which demonstrate what they look like for early childhood education and primary education school leaders. The table also outlines the implications for staff, whānau, and tamariki when these principles are practised effectively in these two settings.

Chapter 1 Walking backwards into the future (Ka mua, ka muri)

Table 1.1 Seven mātauranga Māori principles and values in the education leadership space

How effective Māori leadership can be applied in early childhood and primary school contexts	What this looks like for early childhood education and primary school leaders	Implications for colleagues, whānau, and tamariki in early childhood and primary school when these principles are practised effectively
Whakapapa	Role modelling from the early childhood education and school leader that they understand the importance for Māori of "Ko wai au?" (Who am I?) "Nō hea au?" (Where do I belong?). Incorporate local place-based information in the programme and within the environment (Rātima et al., 2020). Support colleagues, whānau members, and tamariki to connect with and learn about whakapapa, marae, whānau, hapū, and iwi.	Recognition of and value placed on the importance of identity and their culture. A strong sense of belonging. Research illustrates that there is a link between recognition of cultural needs and enhanced learning (Riwai-Couch, 2022).
Whanaungatanga	Strong commitment to Tiriti-based (as opposed to bicultural) practice (Jenkin, 2017; Ritchie & Rau, 2006). Partnership with whānau, hapū, and iwi. Fostering a sense of care, respect, welcome, and hospitality for all members of the school and early childhood centre community (Ritchie & Rau 2006). Respectful and nurturing relationships where individual needs, views, and cultural backgrounds are fostered and prioritised (Riwai-Couch, 2022).	Recognition that te ao Māori and te reo Māori are important and that they are the foundation of everyday Aotearoa. Inclusion of leadership by kaumātua and kuia in your education setting will signal to colleagues, whānau members, and tamariki that they and their whānau are valued and respected.

How effective Māori leadership can be applied in early childhood and primary school contexts	What this looks like for early childhood education and primary school leaders	Implications for colleagues, whānau, and tamariki in early childhood and primary school when these principles are practised effectively
Manaakitanga	Practising rituals; for example, welcomes and farewells and sharing of kai, that reflect te ao Māori (Mead, 2016). Caring for and respecting Māori culture, language values and beliefs including mana and manaakitanga (Education Council New Zealand, 2011). Recognising and developing others' potential including that of colleagues, whānau members, and tamariki, thereby uplifting and strengthening their mana.	Tamariki learn the importance of manaakitanga and practise it with peers, adults, and whānau. Working together as a team to use te reo Māori in practice and showing respect for the culture demonstrates manaakitanga ki te tangata (hospitality and care towards people).
Te reo me ngā tikanga	Supporting the development of te reo me ngā tikanga Māori including with Māori whānau without the expectation that whānau Māori members will lead this (Ritchie & Rau 2006). Avoiding the use of te reo Māori purely for directive purposes (e.g., sit down, listen). This can unintentionally result in it being viewed as "bossy" language, Care needs to be taken that te reo Māori is used for a range of purposes (Ritchie, 2007).	Hearing and observing their own language spoken by others enhances a sense of identity, belonging, and wellbeing for tamariki Māori. The mauri (life force) of te reo and tikanga Māori is supported in daily practices, planning, and programme to ensure tamariki Māori enjoy successful language learning as Māori (Ritchie & Rau, 2006).

How effective Māori leadership can be applied in early childhood and primary school contexts	What this looks like for early childhood education and primary school leaders	Implications for colleagues, whānau, and tamariki in early childhood and primary school when these principles are practised effectively
Aroha	Demonstrating love and care with colleagues, whānau members, and tamariki can be reflected in a range of ways such as listening attentively, sharing, and being kind (Pere, 1997). Walking the talk and ensuring "actions speak louder than words" are particularly important for colleagues, whānau members, and with tamariki. Demonstrating aroha impacts on whanaungatanga and relationships.	When tamariki feel safe and secure in their environment they have an increased tendency to explore, test themselves, and ask questions, all of which impact on learning.
Mauri ora	Mauri ora (life force) is about wellbeing (Durie, 2001). The epitome of mauri ora for Māori is when others enable and support Māori to live and thrive as Māori, recognising their unique values, language, and identity.	When leaders express and show mauri ora, this impacts positively on colleagues, whānau members, and tamariki. Similarly, leaders need to be aware of the mauri ora of colleagues, whānau members, and tamariki and be responsive to their needs (Spiller et al., 2015). Leaders support and develop colleagues, whānau members, and tamariki so that colleagues, whānau members, and tamariki are cognisant of looking after their own and others' mauri.

Conclusion

This chapter, intended for early childhood and primary school leaders, has drawn on seven mātauranga Māori principles to demonstrate how Māori leadership can be enacted in early childhood and primary school settings. The historical context in which these leadership principles have developed has been foregrounded. Contemporary literature and research are used to focus on the implications of practical application of Māori leadership, with a specific emphasis on how colleagues, whānau members, tamariki, and mokopuna will benefit if these principles are effectively practised. There is hope that a bright future awaits our tamariki and mokopuna with the use of the principles outlined in this chapter.

Mahia i runga i te rangimārie me te ngākau māhaki. With a peaceful mind and respectful heart, we will always get the best results.

References

Ballara, A. (1998). *Iwi: The dynamics of Maori tribal organisation from c.1769 to c.1945.* Victoria University Press.

Department of Māori Affairs Te Māori Management Committee. (1988). *Te Māori: He tukunga korero: A report.* Author.

Durie, M. (1998). *Whaiora: Maōri health development* (2nd ed.). Oxford University Press.

Durie, M. (2001). *Mauri ora: The dynamics of Māori health.* Oxford University Press.

Durie, M. (2021). Mātauranga at the interface: An interdisciplinary starter. In J. Ruru & L. W. Nikora (Eds.), *Ngā kete mātauranga: Māori scholars at the research interface* (pp. 22–35). Otago University Press.

Education Council New Zealand. (2011). *Tātaiako: Cultural competencies for teachers of Māori learners.* Ministry of Education. https://teachingcouncil.nz/resource-centre/tataiako-cultural-competencies-for-teachers-of-maori-learners/

Hayward, J. (2004). Te Tiriti o Waitangi: The Treaty of Waitangi. In T. Ka'ai, J. Moorfield, M. Reilly & S. Mosley (Eds.), *Ki te whaiao:Ki te whaiao: An introduction to Māori culture and society* (pp. 151–162). Pearson Education.

Hemara, W. (2000). *Māori pedagogies: A view from literature.* NZCER Press.

Jahnke, H. T. (1997). Towards a theory of mana wahine. *He Pūkenga Kōrero: A Journal of Māori Studies, 3*(1), 27–36.

Jenkin, C. (2017). Early childhood education and biculturalism: Definitions and implications. *New Zealand Journal of Teachers' Work, 14*(1), 8–20. https://doi.org/https://doi.org/10.24135/teacherswork.v14i1.100

Jenkins, K., & Morris Matthews, K. (2005). Mana wahine: Māori women and leadership of Māori schools in Aotearoa/New Zealand. *New Zealand Journal of Education Studies, 40*(1), 45–49.

Ka'ai, T., & Reilly, P. J. (2012). Rangatiratanga: Traditional and contemporary leadership. In T. Ka'ai, J. Moorfield, M. Reilly, & S. Mosley (Eds.), *Ki te whaiao: An introduction to Māori culture and society* (pp. 91–102). Pearson Education.

Katene, S. (2010). Modelling Māori leadership: What makes for good leadership? *MAI Review, 2*, 1–16.

Katene, S. (2013). *The spirit of Māori leadership*. Huia Publishers.

Kelly, D., & Nicholson, A. (2021). Ancestral leadership: Place-based intergenerational leadership. *Leadership, 18*(1), 140–161. http://dx.doi.org/10.1177/17427150211024038

Love, C. (2004). Extensions on te wheke. The Open Polytechnic of New Zealand.

Mead, H. (2016). *Tikanga Māori* (Rev. ed.). Huia Publishers.

Mead, S. M. (1986). *Magnificent te Maori: Te Maori whakahirahira: He korero whakanui i Te Maori*. Heinemann.

Ministry of Education. (2007). *The New Zealand curriculum: For English-medium teaching and learning in years 1–13*. Learning Media. https://nzcurriculum.tki.org.nz/The-New-Zealand-Curriculum

Ministry of Education. (2013). *Ka hikitia—Accelerating success 2013–2017: The Māori education strategy*. https://www.education.govt.nz/assets/Documents/Ministry/Strategies-and-policies/Ka-Hikitia/KaHikitiaAcceleratingSuccessEnglish.pdf

Ministry of Education. (2017). *Te whāriki: He whāriki mātauranga mō ngā mokopuna o Aotearoa: Early childhood curriculum.* Author. https://www.education.govt.nz/assets/Documents/Early-Childhood/Te-Whariki-Early-Childhood-Curriculum-ENG-Web.pdf.

Pere, R. T. (1997). *Te wheke: A celebration of infinite wisdom* (2nd ed.). Ao Ako Global Learning New Zealand.

Pohatu, T. W., & Pohatu, H. (2011). Mauri: Rethinking human wellbeing. *MAI Review, 3*, 1–12.

Rātima, M., Smith, J., MacFarlane, A., & MacFarlane, S. (2020). *The Hikairo schema for primary: Culturally responsive teaching and learning*. NZCER Press.

Ritchie, J. (2007). *Presentation to OMEP*. Presented at the meeting of the Auckland Chapter. OMEP, Auckland.

Ritchie, J., & Rau, C. (2006). Enacting a whakawhanaungatanga approach in early childhood education. *Early Childhood Folio, 10*, 16–20. https://doi.org/10.18296/ecf.0208

Riwai-Couch, M. (2022). *Niho taniwha: Improving teaching and learning for ākonga Māori*. Huia Publishers.

Smith, L. T. (2012). *Decolonizing methodologies research and indigenous people*. Zed Books.

Spiller, C., Barclay-Kerr, H., & Panoho, J. (2015). *Wayfinding leadership: Ground-breaking wisdom for developing leaders*. Huia Publishers.

Summers, T. (2022). *Stories of three female social justice leaders: Understanding the origins of their leadership*. [Doctoral dissertation, University of Canterbury]. http://dx.doi.org/10.26021/13289

Tapiata, R. J., Smith, R., & Akuhata-Brown, M. (2020). *Te kai a te rangatira: Leadership from the Māori world*. Bridget Williams Books.

Te Momo, F. (2011). Whakanekeneke rangatira: Evolving leadership. *MAI Review, 2*, 1–4.

Tuhakaraina, S., & Dayman, T. (2020). Whiria te tangata, whiria te reo Māori: Weaving people, weaving the Māori language. In A. Card & J. Carroll-Lind (Eds.), *Tōku anō reo Māori: My very own language* (pp. 91–100). Te Rito Maioha Early Childhood Education.

Walker, R. (2004). *Ka whawhai tonu matou: Struggle without end* (Rev.ed ed.). Penguin Books.

Williams, N., & Broadley, E. (2012). *Resource kit for tikanga practices.* Ako Aotearoa.

Glossary of te reo Māori terms

ako	teaching and learning
ariki	paramount chief
aroha	love
hapū	sub-tribe
hui	gathering
iwi	tribe or tribal group
kai	food
kaikaranga	the woman who makes the first call on the marae during pōwhiri ritual
kaitiaki	custodians
karanga	a ceremonial call fulfilled by kaikaranga
kaumātua	elders
Kīngitanga	Māori kingdom
kōhanga reo	Māori language nests/preschools
kotahitanga	unity and oneness
kuia	elderly women
kura kaupapa Māori	Māori school
mana	prestige, authority, control, power, influence, status, spiritual power, charisma—mana is a supernatural force in a person, place, or object
manaakitanga	hospitality
manaakitanga ki te tangata	hospitality and care towards people
manuhiri	guests

marae	the open area in front of the wharenui where formal greetings and discussions take place
mātauranga	Māori knowledge
mauri and mauri ora	life force
Papatūānuku	Mother earth
Pākehā	New Zealander of European descent
pepeha	introduction
pūrākau	cultural narrative
tamariki	children
tangata whenua	hosts
tangata whenuatanga	place-based ways of being, doing, and knowing
taonga	treasures/artefacts
te ao Māori	the Māori world
te reo me ngā tikanga	Māori language and protocol
tohunga	expert
tūpuna	ancestors
wahine Māori	Māori woman/women
waiata	song
wānanga	place of learning
whakataukī	proverb
whanaungatanga	relationships, connections
whānau	family
whakapapa	identity
wharenui	meeting house

This glossary has been compiled from Moorfield, J. C. (2003-2022). Te Aka Māori-English, English-Māori Dictionary (https://maoridictionary.co.nz/)

Chapter 2
The distinct nature of Pacific leadership: Applying this within early childhood education and primary schools in Aotearoa New Zealand

Anoop Kumar

Introduction

This chapter focuses on the distinct nature of Pacific leadership and outlines how its principles of this practice can be applied successfully within early childhood education (ECE) and primary school education in Aotearoa New Zealand. First, the chapter outlines the history and nature of Pacific leadership, drawing on literature and examples of leadership within the Pacific cultures. Next, it explains how Pacific people are represented in leadership roles within Aotearoa New Zealand. Later, a framework outlining the four principles of Pacific leadership is presented, followed by a discussion of how these can be applied in ECE and primary leadership and practice. The chapter ends with discussion that is focused on finding a way forward for Pacific leadership in education.

History of Pacific leadership

Traditionally, leadership roles in the Pacific were assigned to chiefs only. The chiefship was incorporated within the concept of the land, which was also used to designate groupings of villages within a broad structure of the Pacific's sociopolitical organisation. Since the arrival of Christian missionaries and the establishment of schools and churches, leadership roles have been taken up by teachers and church leaders who may come from a variety of backgrounds. Subsequently, traditional authority of the chiefs has been undermined due to demographic changes, contributing to increased social and political instability (Veenendaal, 2021).

There has also been a trend of Pacific people immigrating to countries such as Aotearoa New Zealand due to employment opportunities and better lifestyles. Today, Aotearoa New Zealand has a fast-growing population of Pacific people. It is expected to be 20% by 2050 (Ministry of Education, 2018). The increasing presence of Pacific people in Aotearoa New Zealand has had implications for the education of Pacific and non-Pacific children as well as for the Pacific leaders. Pacific leaders in ECE and in primary schools are in a critical position; navigating between two worlds, preserving Pacific culture, promoting aspirations, and protecting the spirituality of the Pacific children and their families.

Representation of Pacific people in leadership roles within Aotearoa New Zealand

Although Pacific peoples are one of the larger ethnic groups in Aotearoa New Zealand, their representation is not reflected in the leadership of our ECE and schools. In this section, the author explores this underrepresentation as well as the strengths that Pacific leaders bring to their role, and challenges for Pacific educational leadership.

Underrepresentation

In Aotearoa New Zealand and other overseas countries, there are a disproportionately small number of teachers and leaders from Pacific backgrounds compared to the number of Pacific students in the communities they serve (Cardno & Auva'a, 2010; Highley, 2023; Van Vooren, 2022). Given this, it is not surprising that research conducted in the United States showed that Pacific students are less likely to encounter a principal from their ethnic background, compared to their white peers (Van Vooren, 2022). Likewise, in recent research conducted in Aotearoa New Zealand, Highley (2023) pointed out that there is limited representation of Pacific leaders in education, which limits opportunities for Pacific voices to be heard. As Highley (2023) argued, because of the lack of a Pacific voice in decision-making spaces, systemic changes to improve outcomes for Pacific learners are limited.

Strengths Pacific people bring to leadership roles

Research demonstrates that Pacific people bring strengths to leadership roles including their rich cultural heritage, passion and commitment to serving their Pacific communities, and empathy for the Pacific students and their families (Cardno & Auva'a, 2010; Highley, 2023). They act as role models and display attributes for a wide range of career and educational choices (Airini, 2010). Maiava-Zajkowski (2021) argues that young Pacific people are more motivated to succeed when they see role models from their culture in leadership.

Highley (2023) claimed that, while Pacific leaders are humble and passionate about the Pacific communities, they have a commitment to serve their community over and beyond what is expected. Pacific leaders can easily interpret situations in a Pacific way because they understand the culture and heritage of the families they work with. This is supported by the Ministry of Education (2020) which pointed out that, for Pacific communities in Aotearoa New Zealand, it is important to have "teachers and leaders who can easily relate to and empathise with diverse Pacific learners" (p. 38).

Furthermore, Pacific leaders bring with them traditional protocol tools such as *talanoa* (free-flowing conversation between people), that can be applied in relationship building and connecting with their Pacific communities. Vaioleti (2006) describes talanoa as talking in an informal way to tell stories and relate experiences. Through talanoa, Pacific leaders also act as advocates and support persons for others at meetings.

Challenges faced by Pacific people in leadership roles

Despite the strengths they bring to leadership roles, studies have shown Pacific people in these roles face challenges regarding their gender and ethnicity, career opportunities, and lack of support from management (Cardno & Auva'a, 2010; Dalli & Thornton, 2013; Highley, 2023). Traditional approaches to leadership continue to discourage females and Indigenous practitioners from associating themselves with the notion of leadership (Dalli & Thornton, 2013). This means that gender and ethnicity can act as barriers for Pacific leaders in a society dominated by Western ways of knowing and doing. It implies that such cultural norms may contribute to low recruitment rates of Pacific leaders in workplaces (Cardno & Auva'a, 2010).

Another challenge many Pacific leaders face in Aotearoa New Zealand is English being their second language. Moodley (2016), in her study of Pacific ECE teachers, pointed out that English language was a significant barrier for Pacific teachers to pursue leadership positions in ECE. Moodley found that Pacific teachers faced difficulties in writing reports, communications with board members at meetings, and articulating their professional knowledge in English to external professional agencies such as Education Review officers. This suggests that problems with English may cause miscommunication and confusion among the teaching team. A further challenge for Pacific people in leadership roles is that they find it difficult to progress and, as a result, their voices are not represented or heard at decision-making levels (Maiava-Zajkowski, 2021).

A framework for Pacific leadership

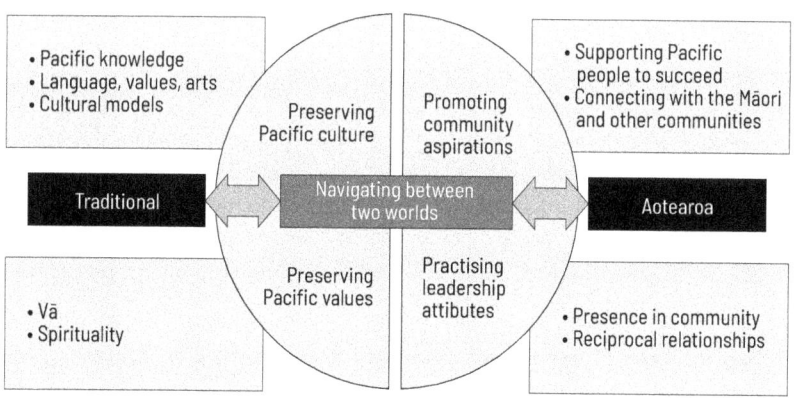

Figure 2.1 Principles of Pacific leadership

This section presents and discusses a framework, designed by the author, that demonstrates the distinct nature of Pacific leadership. Included in the framework are the following four key principles: preserving Pacific culture; promoting community aspirations; practising leadership attributes; and protecting the *vā* (sacred relationships between people) and spirituality (see Figure 2.1).

Preserving Pacific culture

Ioane (2017) pointed out that the survival of the Pacific culture and its identity is still fundamentally based on understanding the traditional values, culture, and histories of each nation in Aotearoa New Zealand. This means that leaders in ECE and primary schools have an important role to ensure the preservation of their culture; maintaining cultural practices, language, identity, and arts; and passing cultural knowledge from one generation to another. In Aotearoa New Zealand, Pacific languages, traditional music and dance, and food and religious practices are celebrated during the annual Pasifika Festival. This event gathers people from Pacific countries to present Pacific cultures through traditional activities, food, and dance performances, to bring awareness to younger generations. However, this may not be enough to preserve the Pacific culture. Pacific school leaders will need to play a critical role in promoting and nurturing the Pacific culture in order to avoid the real risk of losing it.

Ministry of Education documents, including *Tapasā* (2018), *Te Whāriki* (2017), and *Action Plan for Pacific Education 2020–2030* (2020), have been created for all teachers of Pacific children to establish, build, and grow their understanding of Pacific ways of being and doing. Van Vooren (2022) pointed out that candidates for leadership positions display more confidence if the senior leadership supports the process and shows belief in their skills.

In Pacific culture, teacher-leaders are viewed as custodians of Pacific culture and are expected to ensure that core Pacific knowledge, values, and beliefs are passed on to future generations. Leaders can achieve this through initiatives such as applying cultural models to guide discussions and decisions about the curriculum. For example, the Falalalaga (Samoan) and Fale Hanga (Tongan) models that focus on mat weaving are perceived as the way Pacific children are raised. Therefore, creating and displaying these tangible cultural models in classrooms give meaning and identity to the Pacific people. Seeing, touching, and talking about these cultural models (mats) are likely to generate stories of the struggles and successes of the Pacific people in Aotearoa. Secondly, teachers can make deliberate attempts to ensure the Pacific language is visible in their dialogues with children, parents, and the community. For example, greeting the Pacific children and their families in their language is in congruence with the principles of *Tapasā* (Ministry of Education, 2018) which state that a good teacher understands that identity, culture, and language are important.

Promoting community aspirations

The key aspirations of the Pacific community in Aotearoa New Zealand are for learners to feel safe, valued, and equipped to achieve their education aspirations (Ministry of Education, 2020). Pacific people aspire to share and celebrate with other communities their language, cultures, and identities which are vital to their sense of wellbeing and to their future. Pacific people know that, if their aspirations are not understood, then the journey of their communities and their cultures is likely to diminish. Therefore, Pacific leaders in schools and ECE centres are seen as the guardians who will understand and support the aspirations of their greater community.

Chu-Fuluifaga and Reynolds (2023) suggested that changes in educational practice, both individually and institutionally, are required to unpack these aspirations. This implies that leaders within ECE and schools may be operating in disconnect to the aspirations of Pacific children, families, and communities. To help bridge the gap, the Ministry of Education has provided numerous initiatives for teachers and school leaders. One such initiative is development of *Tapasā*. The *Tapasā* framework brings Pacific perspectives to effective and quality teaching practice at different stages of a teacher's journey (Ministry of Education, 2018). The framework also supports teachers of non-Pacific identity to be equipped to connect and go beyond the surface, when learning and working alongside Pacific children and their families.

In addition, it is important for ECE and school leaders to foster connections with local Māori and other communities in Aotearoa New Zealand. Pacific leaders will need to work in collaboration with other social institutions, such as marae, and with concepts such as mana whenua, to reaffirm the importance of maintaining their strongly rooted cultures (Cardno & Auva'a, 2010). Pacific and Māori communities socialise in churches and on marae; these places can become vital partner institutions in networking and celebrating their culture away from their island nations. Sports, festivals, and *fono* (meetings) are other opportunities leaders may use to promote aspirations and interactions of Pacific people with other communities.

Practising leadership attributes

A key element of Pacific school leaders is their ability to integrate their communities into their schools and ECE centres. Sanga et al. (2022) identified two attributes of Pacific leaders that may contribute ways to operationalise their leadership with the communities. These address the significance of presence and the effect of reciprocal relationships on the part of leaders.

First, the physical presence of Pacific school leaders in their wider school community is likely to contribute to the significance of their leadership in Aotearoa New Zealand. In the Pacific context, the life of a school leader is very transparent because people don't see any division between the leader's personal life and their professional life. What Pacific leaders do after hours is accounted for by their community as well as what they do inside the classroom. This explains why a Pacific leader's community presence can maintain consistency of their actions in their official role and their leadership in daily life. Sanga et al. (2022) point out that a Pacific school leader may have authority in the classroom, but their leadership requires sanctioned behaviour in a range of other community contexts, including family and church. Sanga et al. (2022) caution that a narrow institutional conception of leadership may mute the holistic nature of Pacific societies and erode the integration of education and community.

Secondly, reciprocal relationships underpin Pacific worldviews and cultural practices (Tamasese et al., 2010) and Pacific leaders prefer working reciprocally with Pacific communities to respond to their unmet needs. Reciprocity involves a mutually beneficial exchange of support that makes each person feel cared for and loved. Pacific leaders in schools understand what works best for Pacific students. Therefore, it is important for them to set expectations for schools and to work to support the integration of school and the community. Working together with Pacific parents and other teachers is likely to make a difference for communities. Pacific leaders can strengthen this collaboration through parent–teacher meetings and training workshops to inform teachers, parents, and community leaders about their roles and responsibilities. Parent–teacher associations can provide a forum where respectful exchange of views and information-sharing and understandings may cement school–community relationships. Such reciprocal relations and community contributions place value on education beyond the institutions.

Protecting Pacific values

"Pacific" comprises a multitude of Pacific nations, but there are commonalities in values across them. Key among the values are the *vā* (sacred relationships between people) and spirituality. The Pacific community considers their leaders in ECE and schools accountable to nurture and protect these non-negotiable values.

Finau et al. (2022) define vā as representing an in-depth understanding and respect that is shown by one Pacific person to another through the connections of the space between people and things. Similarly, Matapo and McFall-McCaffery (2022) explain vā as a Pacific Indigenous philosophical concept which is a central feature that grounds all relationships and connections. The vā is always present in and around. Among Pacific peoples, the vā defines their collective past, present, and future. When the vā is not respected, it may result in disharmony within a relationship. The concept of vā brings a rich understanding of how Pacific leaders view their environments as part of relationship building. Pacific people nurture the concept of vā naturally and in everyday situations, even in schools and ECE settings. Yet when placed within a Western environment, the concept of vā may be misunderstood and can lead to the disruption of relationships between Western leaders and Pacific people. It is the responsibility of Pacific school leaders to ensure that vā is not only protected but promoted for the success of Pacific identity in Aotearoa New Zealand.

Another key value of the Pacific community is spirituality. A vast majority of Pacific people are spiritual and believe in God. Since the arrival of Christian missionaries in the Island nations, churches have provided spiritual guidance and protocols. The church remains current and relevant for many Pacific peoples in Aotearoa New Zealand. The Pacific community in Aotearoa New Zealand wants this belief to be nurtured and maintained within young children. An example of this is opening meetings in schools with a prayer and starting and ending the day with a prayer. The blessing of food is important to many Pacific learners. It is essential to create environments in schools and ECE centres that are safe and supportive of Pacific learners with regards to their spiritual faith and life experiences. Pacific learners value their spiritual faith and particularly the Christian faith, which is a vital part of their lives.

The way forward

It is clear that Pacific leaders in ECE and schools encounter multiple complexities that need to be navigated. Their ways of knowing and being may be contrary to the Western way of life, which may confuse many in Aotearoa New Zealand. This contradiction often puts pressure on Pacific leaders in the education sector to navigate between their traditional ways of being and professional leadership expectation in ECE settings and schools. The author offers three suggestions as a way forward for Pacific leaders.

Firstly, Pacific leaders have rich cultural wealth and need to believe in their own ability to perform in leadership roles. Airini (2010) suggests that certain personal attributes can contribute to effective leadership. These include, "stamina not to give up, preference to be in leadership roles, recognised desire, and skill to motivate others, confidence and ability to attempt something new, a sense of peace and assurance" (p. 11).

Secondly, it is essential to have leadership training programmes to promote the values and customs of both the Pacific and the non-Pacific groups represented in Aotearoa New Zealand. Hattori (2016) argues that it is important for a Pacific person to develop competence as an "authentic" leader by "identifying, articulating and practicing" their culture (p. 1) and aligning values with actions.

Thirdly, it is evident that Pacific leaders need to develop support networks. Brown (2019) indicates that support networks and systems are important for Pacific teachers and aspiring leaders. Pacific school leaders in Aotearoa could look at establishing a wider regional and global network. Such a network will need to ensure that the agenda of quality culturally responsive pedagogies, Pacific languages, and cultural values and beliefs are well articulated to wider education.

Conclusion

Pacific leadership in the context of ECE and primary schools in Aotearoa New Zealand requires attention. There are a growing number of Pacific people, yet there is a small number of Pacific leaders in schools and ECE settings, leading to underrepresentation of the voices of Pacific people in Aotearoa New Zealand. The framework of Pacific leadership put forward by the author outlines four principles that are all action-focused and important to understand. Alongside these principles, the *Action Plan for Pacific Education 2020–2030* (Ministry of Education, 2020) also calls for a commitment to grow, retain, and value highly competent Pacific teachers and leaders and emphasises that every leader and educational professional needs to take coordinated action to become culturally competent with diverse Pacific learners. The plan further calls on leaders to partner with families and other teachers to design education opportunities together so that aspirations for learning can be met.

Finally, it is time to acknowledge and value the distinct nature of Pacific leadership. It is critical we support the contribution of Pacific leaders in ECE and primary sectors in Aotearoa New Zealand. It is my hope that this chapter will inspire readers to understand the dilemma Pacific leaders in education sectors may be in while navigating between two worlds in Aotearoa New Zealand.

References

Airini. (2010). "Be true to one's self": Learning to be leaders in Pasifika education strategy. *MAI Review, 2010*(1), 1–22. https://journal.mai.ac.nz/system/files/maireview/308-2291-1-PB.pdf

Brown, M. (2019). *Educational leadership through a Pasifika lens: Navigating their way in a New Zealand secondary school context* [Master of Educational Leadership thesis, Auckland University of Technology]. http://hdl.handle.net/10292/12969

Cardno, C., & Auva'a, E. (2010). A study of Pacific Island senior managers as aspiring principals in New Zealand primary schools. *International Studies in Educational Administration, 38*(2), 86–99.

Chu-Fuluifaga, C., & Reynolds, M. (2023). Pursuing educational partnerships in diasporic contexts: Teachers responding to Pacific voice in their work. *Merits, 3*, 351–365. https://doi.org/10.3390/merits3020020

Dalli, C., & Thornton, K. (2013). Professionalism and leadership. In D. Pendergast & S. Garvis, *Teaching early years: Curriculum, pedagogy and assessment* (pp. 303–316). Allen & Unwin.

Finau, S. P., Paea, M. K., & Reynolds, M. (2022). Pacific people navigating the sacred vā to frame relational care: A conversation between friends across space and time. *The Contemporary Pacific, 34*(1). https://doi.org/10.1353/cp.2022.0006

Hattori, M. (2016). Culturally sustaining leadership: A Pacific Islander's perspective. *Education Sciences, 6*(1), 1–10. https://doi.org/10.3390/educsci6010004

Highley, V. (2023). Valuing, growing and retaining Pacific leaders and teachers. *Kairaranga, 24*(1), 19–32. https://doi.org/10.54322/kairaranga.v24i1.353

Ioane, J. (2017). Talanoa with Pasifika youth and their families. *New Zealand Journal of Psychology, 46*(3), 38–45. https://www.psychology.org.nz/journal-archive/Talanoa-with-Pasifika-youth-and-their-families-private.pdf

Maiava-Zajkowski, R. (2021). *Realising Pacific potential in Aotearoa New Zealand: Occupational segregation and pathways to leadership.* Manatū Wāhine.

Matapo, J., & McFall-McCaffery, J. T. (2022). Towards a vā knowledge ecology: Mobilising Pacific philosophy to transform higher education for Pasifika in Aotearoa New Zealand. *Journal of Higher Education Policy and Management, 44*(2), 122–137. https://doi.org/10.1080/1360080X.2022.2041258

Ministry of Education. (2018). *Tapasā: Cultural competencies framework for teachers of Pacific learners.* https://teachingcouncil.nz/resource-centre/tapasa/

Ministry of Education. (2020). *Action plan for Pacific education 2020-2030.* https://conversation.education.govt.nz/conversations/action-plan-for-pacific-education/

Moodley, E. (2016). *Leadership in early childhood education: The journey of Pasifika educators* [Master's thesis, Auckland University of Technology].

Sanga, K., Johansson-Fua, S., Reynolds, M., Fa'avae, D., Robyns, R., Rohoana, G., Hiele, G., Jim, D., Case, L. J., & Malachi, D. (2022). The context behind the context: A Pacific leadership research "tok stori". *International Education Journal: Comparative Perspectives, 21*(2), 5-20. https://openjournals.library.sydney.edu.au/IEJ/article/view/15912

Tamasese, K, Parsons, L, Sullivan, G & Waldegrave, C. (2010). *A Qualitative Study into Pacific Perspectives of Cultural Obligations and Volunteering.* Family Centre Social Policy Research Unit.

Vaioleti, T. M. (2006). Talanoa research methodology: A developing position on Pacific research. *Waikato Journal of Education, 12,* 21–34. https://doi.org/10.15663/wje.v12i1.296

Van Vooren, C. (2022). Urgency in our schools. *Leadership Magazine,* March–April 2022. https://leadership.acsa.org/urgency-in-our-schools

Veenendaal, W. (2021). How instability creates stability: The survival of democracy in Vanuatu. *Third World Quarterly, 42*(6), 1330–1346. https://doi.org/10.1080/01436597.2021.1890577

Chapter 3
Systems-convening leadership and cross-sector collaboration

Tiffany Williams

Introduction

Leadership that supports collaboration creates space for people to draw on their expertise, share knowledge, and develop a shared vision for improvement. Those in leadership roles have a profound impact on collaborative efforts within or across education sectors, supporting teachers to work together and bridge gaps in knowledge and practice. For teachers in early childhood education (ECE) and primary sectors in Aotearoa New Zealand, there are opportunities to cross their siloed contexts (Kamp, 2019; New Appointments National Panel [NANP], 2021) through Kāhui Ako | Communities of Learning, an initiative that explicitly calls for cross-sector collaboration and developing teacher leadership (Rawlins et al., 2014). The initiative includes explicit opportunities for teachers to lead across contexts, working in "the spaces between schools" (Kamp, 2019, p. 182) to highlight teacher expertise in different schools and centres. However, for cross-sector collaboration to occur, both contexts must enjoy a particular kind of leadership that supports the sharing of diverse ideas and expertise. Leaders who facilitate collaboration by embracing the border between contexts, rather than seeking sameness (Williams, 2023), encourage other teachers and leaders in cross-sector contexts to do the same.

Wenger-Trayner and Wenger-Trayner (2024) have defined a cross-sector leadership style as "systems-convening", for people who seek connection with other experts and want to solve problems of practice in a social way. Without a term to define this approach to leadership, it can seem messy or disruptive, as systems conveners often find themselves outside what is normally done. Systems conveners see immense value in collaborating with people outside their usual contexts, drawing on fresh expertise and wider perspectives. A systems convener tends to be somewhat of an expert in their usual context, with a high level of knowledge and experience relevant to the wider community (Wenger-Trayner & Wenger-Trayner, 2021). Because of this knowledge and experience, they not only have a good understanding of the issues that community members are facing, but they are also able to use knowledge of their community to help them bring about sustainable change.

Often the impact of systems-convening work is recognised in retrospect, if it is recognised at all (Wenger-Trayner & Wenger-Trayner, 2021). However, this style of leadership has been explicitly mandated in Aotearoa New Zealand as part of the Kāhui Ako initiative. Originally focused on secondary and primary schools, the potential for ECE involvement in Kāhui Ako was developed in late 2014 (NANP, 2021). Kāhui Ako vary in size, ranging from four schools to 20 schools (Wylie, 2016), with some co-located Kāhui Ako combining their work to foster collaboration across a town and city (Williams, 2023). Their work is focused on broad goals referred to as "achieve challenges", which are based on localised data of students across schools (Constantinides & Eleftheriadou, 2023). New leadership positions were developed as part of the Kāhui Ako initiative including lead principals, across school leads, and within school leads. Teachers appointed to any of these three leadership roles were focused on supporting their Kāhui Ako to work towards the realisation of their achieve challenges and address change in education at all levels, from governance to the classroom.

However, as research has shown, simply creating leadership positions and mandating collaboration (Kamp, 2019) does not necessarily equate to successful collaborative practice (e.g., Boyle & Petriwskyj, 2014; Sinnema et al., 2021; Wylie, 2016). The research that informs this chapter was undertaken to explore how leadership within Kāhui Ako supports cross-sector collaboration. Systems-convening leadership emerged from the study as being an effective way forward for Kāhui

Ako, whether leaders held a position title or not. The chapter provides an outline of the study, followed by the findings that are presented and discussed under three headings derived from the data. Finally, a conclusion is provided.

The study

Nine teachers from one Kāhui Ako each participated in individual interviews. The individual teachers are referred to in this chapter with P (participant) followed by a letter. These participants included three each from the key education sectors of ECE, primary, and secondary. The nine participants held a wide range of leadership positions, including head teachers, deans, school principals, and senior teachers, as well as within school leads, across school leads, and lead principals in their Kāhui Ako. The teaching experience of the participants ranged from 6 years to 42 years. While some had been involved in the establishment of the Kāhui Ako approximately 5 years before the research occurred, other participants had been involved for less than a year. Following the individual interviews, data were thematically analysed. This analysis highlighted the strong influence of systems-convening leadership on effective cross-sector collaboration.

Although not all the participants practised a systems-convening style of leadership, they all observed aspects of this leadership approach within other Kāhui Ako members. Specifically, participants talked about how the leadership of their Kāhui Ako supported them to engage in cross-sector collaboration by drawing on effective leadership attributes and encouraging the same attributes in others. The research found that systems-convening leaders—that is, the Kāhui Ako members who demonstrated strong systems-convening attributes—facilitated understanding of the border between contexts in three distinct ways. First, they communicated a clear vision for improvement; second, they intentionally fostered a collaborative community built on relational trust; and third, they encouraged the sharing of diverse teacher expertise. The findings are presented and discussed next, alongside relevant literature, under these headings.

Communicating a clear vision for improvement

A major factor in systems-convening leadership is communicating a clear vision for improvement. Communicating a clear vision for improvement was a key approach for systems conveners in the Kāhui Ako to promote understanding of the borders between education contexts. Indeed, a lead principal of the participating Kāhui Ako stated, "I always believed, if you've got a really strong rationale for your community about why you are doing something, then you should actually have the courage to stand up for that and stick with it" (PL). Leaders who have communicated a clear vision for improvement promote an understanding of the border as a place to connect with others who are also seeking improvement. The goal is not to make everyone think the same, but to capitalise on the diversity of people to approach a shared "problem of practice" (PC and PL). For the participating Kāhui Ako, this was made clear by PL who believed, "We should be able to develop around our own uniqueness, around the children, but still have this common goal of actually improving education for the region".

Indeed, improving education for the region was the vision for improvement for the participating Kāhui Ako. PK, for example, asserted that "it is not about finding outcomes that suit me or necessarily an outcome that suits schools, although those are fundamentally and essentially important. But we're all talking about the learner. I want 'the learner' to be the pivotal conversation." For her, cross-sector collaboration provided an opportunity to "tie together a lot of important thinking about the essential ingredients that nurture success for learners". For any community of learners or practice, the vision for improvement is a call to people who are seeking change, perhaps seeking revolution, and are not afraid to go about that in a unique or revolutionary way (Wenger-Trayner & Wenger-Trayner, 2024). It was evident from the findings that all the participants were passionate about the vision of their Kāhui Ako, being the learning and wellbeing of learners across classrooms and beyond.

Furthermore, there was a keen sense of "getting it right for our kids … because they're all in our community" (PE). As PW explained, "If cross-sector collaboration is happening really well, then we are doing the best by children and their families". Many of the participants shared an understanding of learners not just as members of a classroom, but as members of the wider community they shared with teachers. Their shared vision for improvement meant they saw the border between sectors as a chance to connect with others who were also wanting to support all learners as contributing members of society. This is the motivation for any systems convener; they want to effect positive change for people in the community they are a part of (Wenger-Trayner & Wenger-Trayner, 2024). By working together across borders, the members of the Kāhui Ako showed they were able to achieve their vision.

With a clear vision for educational improvement, teachers from all sectors within the Kāhui Ako had the opportunity to see themselves in the vision and to contribute. Their vision for improvement included a broad, but shared, understanding of what success looked like, focusing firmly on wellbeing and being responsive to community needs. PW explained that the shared vision for improvement went a long way to address "a number of deficit lenses on our young people in the community". PC shared a similar view: "I think if all the layers of the community are doing well and thriving and successful, then we all benefit from that". Herein lies evidence of a systems-convener's desire to address problems of practice in their full complexity through collaboration with diverse people (Wenger-Trayner & Wenger-Trayner, 2021). PK, a teacher in ECE, felt this to be true of the leaders in the Kāhui Ako who demonstrated systems-convening attributes, stating: "I absolutely know that they are committed to the conversations, and the involvement of us all". Leaders ensured their community members knew that collaborative work was open to everyone, and sustainable change relied on the involvement of all sectors.

Building a collaborative culture built on relational trust

Another way leaders in the Kāhui Ako encouraged varied understandings of the borders between contexts was to build a collaborative culture that included teachers from all education sectors. To do this, the research found that leaders actively fostered relational trust between

Kāhui Ako members who came to see the border between sectors as a source of community and professional support. For example, PC talked at length about the collaborative culture, which was "the power of the Kāhui Ako". PE found the Kāhui Ako "an empowering space". This was echoed by PK, who believed in the Kāhui Ako community's "commitment to working together" and that their "relationship connections are based on mutual goodwill". These findings highlight that, because of systems-convening leadership, the border becomes a place of collegial support (Clark, 2018). Teachers can discuss challenges or celebrate achievements with others who are also invested in building stronger collegial relationships.

Leaders in Kāhui Ako were able to build a collaborative culture across borders by fostering relational trust. Relational trust is where people "maintain both an understanding of their own role obligations, and expectations about the obligations of others" (Sinnema et al., 2021, p. 35). For the participants, fostering relational trust meant they needed to learn about the work occurring in other sectors. For example, PC saw effective cross-sector collaboration when principals and teachers said to each other, "I want to know about you and your world, and how that works in your school." It meant that teachers would be "coming from a place of genuine understanding, wanting to seek understanding, rather than this is me in my school and it's done like this" (PC). The openness required for the development of relational trust was also mentioned by other research participants. PM felt he had "grown a lot and changed [through] honest, collaborative learning". Similarly, PH celebrated the excitement of "people just having radical honesty and growing … people who wouldn't normally work together … are sharing knowledge and making a difference". With consistent attention to developing relational trust, the participants were able to see the impact their relationship-building work was having. It was not just understanding each other's work but influencing each other's work through their collaboration as well.

Nonetheless, the participants understood that establishing relational trust and a collaborative culture took time and effort. PK, for example, explained they (the Kāhui Ako members) knew that "collaborative relationships and working together, things like that, we need to always keep working on". The research found that leaders who displayed systems-convening attributes also knew the development of relational trust takes time, so they actively protected that time for Kāhui Ako members. PH described the phenomenon as a "curve" because the leaders in the Kāhui Ako "started off slow but once that relationship was solidified, there's almost nothing we can't have a go at now". Participants who were also leaders in the Kāhui Ako acknowledged this time. PL explained that "getting people to understand collaboration was a big part of our work when we first started out … [collaboration] is a really misunderstood term". The early work on developing a shared understanding also helped addressed the "competitive silos" of school mentioned by Participants S, C, T, and E. In addition, PE discussed the building of relational trust between ECE and primary school teachers through regular meetings. She explained the group of teachers "spent a year working pretty hard to build the relationship … and there were definitely ups and downs. The collaboration has come into play, but it was hard to get there". The establishment of relational trust was shown in the study to be essential for teachers to collaborate across the ECE/primary school border.

Sharing of diverse teacher expertise

The study highlighted how leaders within the Kāhui Ako recognised diverse teacher expertise and deliberately promoted this across contexts. Indeed, as PL, a lead principal in the Kāhui Ako, asserted:

> There's a lot of knowledge and expertise in an area that just goes untapped. We buy in all this outside expertise, when actually, we don't need to. [Cross-sector collaboration] is about surfacing the expertise and growing the profession from the ground up.

This example is indicative of another essential trait of systems-convening. Not only are systems conveners focused on embracing diverse expertise, they also know that change can only be achieved if people are willing to contribute their expertise to a shared vision for change (Wenger-Trayner & Wenger-Trayner, 2021).

The study showed that teachers in the Kāhui Ako came to see the border as a sort of resource bank, where they could gather ideas, tools, and knowledge. This is important because teachers may not completely understand the broader, more complex vision for improvement, or perhaps the sense of relational trust needed to engage in a genuinely collaborative culture. Seeing the border as an opportunity to gain fresh ideas for the classroom was perhaps the strongest understanding developed in Kāhui Ako, encouraging a wide range of teachers to connect across various sectors. The findings showed that recognition of diverse teacher expertise, and intentionally highlighting this expertise for the broad audience of Kāhui Ako membership, was an important step in encouraging the wider community to engage with the borders between contexts. Teachers were able to learn about each other, using shared interests in practice as common ground. This aligns with the work of Boyle and Petriwskyj (2014) and Bond et al. (2019) who contend mutual understanding of each other's work needs to be developed in order to engage in genuine cross-sector collaboration.

For the Kāhui Ako, developing an understanding of expertise across contexts was essential for "narrowing the gap" (PT) between ECE and primary sectors. This gap was described by PE as "a giant abyss" before intentional, ongoing sharing of ideas and perspective was facilitated between ECE and primary teachers. Teachers from both ECE and primary sectors were able to work on creating "the relationships [needed] between ECE and primary for transitions" (PT). This inevitably included the sharing of curriculum and pedagogy expertise, as well as the formation of lasting professional networks. This example aligns research by Bond et al. (2019) and Clark (2018) who propose transitions can be used as a shared interest to engage with others across contexts. Having a shared interest, such as transitions, can be essential in establishing purpose for teachers who otherwise may not see any benefit in cross-sector collaboration. Shared interests can also support teachers who may hold particular beliefs about another sector that acts as a barrier. PS acknowledged these barriers: "I guess it does take—it will take a bit of knocking down stereotypes, even I am guilty of it." PL saw these assumptions in Kāhui Ako members, too, and actively promoted engagement at the border to address them: "I hear teachers say,

'If only early childhood did this'. So I say, 'Let's go and visit the early childhood centre'." For many of the participants, sharing ideas with a teacher from another education sector was essential in addressing assumptions held about different contexts.

By supporting the sharing of diverse expertise across borders, Kāhui Ako leaders were helping teachers recognise their own skills. Indeed, because systems-conveners are drawn to the border where diversity thrives, they often possess skills and knowledge that are useful across contexts (Wenger-Trayner & Wenger-Trayner, 2021). PH certainly appreciated the ability to take "big, cool ideas" and work with teachers they would not ordinarily get to meet, to find a way to bring those ideas to life. PL also explained that many teachers in the Kāhui Ako "are leading change in their own school. They are also leading change in the Kāhui Ako. Some are working with other schools, which has been really exciting." Similarly, PH recognised he "was learning so much from sharing" through the within-school lead role, which contributed to his growing leadership capability: "I was just a 'scale A' teacher, but it was a really cool time in my career … I already had those 'big cool ideas', but I grew a lot". Teachers who come to recognise their own expertise and are supported to share it with others begin to demonstrate their own systems-convening attributes (Wenger-Trayner & Wenger-Trayner, 2021). They also come to appreciate the border as a place of learning and innovation.

Conclusion

Systems-convening leadership provided a startlingly accurate description of the actions and attributes of the leaders in this study who actively crossed borders between education contexts in the Kāhui Ako. However, it is important to note they did not learn about systems-convening; they were compelled by a desire to improve and were motivated by the success of their learners. Learning about effective cross-sector collaboration with the Kāhui Ako was like seeing Wenger-Trayner and Wenger-Trayner's (2021) assertion in action; that in order to respond to challenges, growth, and change, communities require systems-convening leadership.

When leaders intentionally promote varied understandings of the border, cross-sector collaboration can become an appealing professional opportunity for teachers for a variety of reasons. This includes teachers who have a strong vision for improvement, enjoy a sense of community and connection, want fresh ideas for their classroom, or want to work on something specific, such as transition to school from ECE. Leaders who want to foster collaborative spaces see all these understandings as valid. Furthermore, leaders know that, once teachers are engaging with the border, their individual understandings can be built and diversified. Systems-convening leadership has been found to support these varied understandings of the border. Systems convening encourages teachers to embrace the border as an opportunity to engage in cross-sector collaboration and improve educational success for themselves and their learners. Therefore, this style of leadership provides exciting opportunities for collaborative teaching and learning communities such as Kāhui Ako in Aotearoa New Zealand. With further understanding of systems-convening leadership and its purposeful application, teachers in ECE and primary education can realise sustainable change in their sectors through collaboration, innovation, and strong cross-sector relationships.

References

Bond, L., Brown, J., Hutchings, J., & Peters, S. (2019). A collaborative approach to transitions in Dannevirke. *Early Childhood Folio, 23*(2), 18–23. https://doi.org/10.18296/ecf.0066

Boyle, T., & Petriwskyj, A. (2014). Transitions to school: Reframing professional relationships. *Early Years, 34*(4), 392–404. https://doi.org/10.1080/09575146.2014.953042

Clark, M. (2018). Edges and boundaries: Finding community and innovation as an early childhood educator. *Early Childhood Education Journal, 47,* 153–162. https://doi.org/10.1007/s10643-018-0904-z

Constantinides, M., & Eleftheriadou, S. (2023). The role of leadership in communities of learning | Kāhui Ako: A systematic literature review. *New Zealand Journal of Education Studies, 58,* 341–359. https://doi.org/10.1007/s40841-023-00295-2

Kamp, A. (2019). Kāhui Ako and the collaborative turn in education: Emergent evidence and leadership implications. *New Zealand Annual Review of Education, 24,* 177–191. https://doi.org/10.26686/nzaroe.v24i0.6493

New Appointments National Panel. (2021). *Collaborative practice emerging across Kāhui Ako: Ten trends.* Education Counts. https://www.educationcounts.govt.nz/publications/schooling2/workforce/collaborative-practice-emerging-across-kahui-ako-ten-trends

Rawlins, P., Ashton, K., Carusi, T. & Lewis, E. (2014). *Investing in educational success: An investigation of the evidence base.* NZEI Te Riu Roa.

Sinnema, C., Hannah, D., Finnerty, A., & Daly, A. (2021). A theory of action account of an across-school collaboration policy in practice. *Journal of Educational Change, 23,* 33–60. https://doi.org/10.1007/s10833-020-09408-w

Wenger-Trayner, B., & Wenger-Trayner, E. (2021). *Systems convening: A crucial form of leadership for the 21st century.* Social Learning Lab.

Wenger-Trayner, B., & Wenger-Trayner, E. (2024). *Systems convening: The art of convening diverse voice across difficult boundaries.* https://www.wenger-trayner.com/systems-convening/

Williams, T. (2023). *Crossing the border: Supporting factors of collaboration in one Kāhui Ako.* [Master's thesis, Te Rito Maioha Early Childhood New Zealand]. Open Polytech Kuratini Tuwhera Library and Learning Centre. https://library.openpolytechnic.ac.nz/record=b2868028

Wylie, C. (2016). *Communities of learning / Kāhui Ako: The emergent stage. Findings from the NZCER national survey of primary and intermediate schools 2016.* New Zealand Council for Educational Research—Rangahau Mātauranga o Aotearoa. https://www.nzcer.org.nz/research/publications/communities-learning-emergent-stage

Chapter 4

Navigating emotional responses to educational change: Empowering leaders through knowledge and action

Beth Germaine

Introduction

Despite the pervasive presence of emotions, their significance in the context of educational change is not something routinely explored by leaders in educational contexts. Even highly relational leaders may not fully grasp the nuanced emotional landscape of change settings and how feelings of uncertainty and risk can profoundly influence the experiences of individuals involved in change initiatives. Consequently, when educational leaders encounter emotions in the form of tears, tantrums, or stonewalling and silence, they are frequently caught off-guard and can be left feeling ill-equipped to navigate these emotional dynamics as leaders (Timperley et al., 2020).

Fortunately, with knowledge and action it is possible to transform the emotional experience of change into a more positive and manageable process. This chapter aims to empower leaders to do this by helping them to make sense of the role that emotions have in a complex change process and identify leadership actions that can be taken to help navigate emotional responses effectively.

As an experienced educator and leader in a primary school setting in Aotearoa New Zealand, the author has a personal interest in understanding why the process of educational change can be so difficult for those involved. The ideas and recommendations in this chapter draw from their review of relevant Aotearoa New Zealand-based literature and research conducted as part of their Master's research on emotions in educational change.

The chapter first discusses the complex nature of change in educational settings and how this contributes to the emergence of emotions such as feelings of vulnerability and risk. Next, it explores current thinking about how a "perceptions of risk" lens can help leaders make sense of and respond to the range of emotions that they and their teachers may experience as part of the change process. Next, a framework for navigating emotional responses, which has been drawn from literature, is presented (Table 4.1). This framework comprises interconnecting strategies and actions that leaders can use to help them, and their teachers navigate the emotions and the sense of vulnerability that are inherent in educational change. This chapter ends with a conclusion.

A note: The research about feelings of vulnerability and perceptions of risk that this chapter draws from is based in the context of professional learning. Therefore, when talking about educational change, the author is specifically referring to cycles of school improvement that relate to learning and teaching. The terms "educational change", "professional learning", and "change initiatives" have been used interchangeably to refer to the range of activities that leaders and teachers engage in as part of their efforts to improve student outcomes.

Emotional responses to change in educational settings

Although the body of knowledge and research about change processes and teaching practices that work is increasing, making change in educational settings "stick" remains frustratingly elusive (Timperley et al., 2020). One reason for this is that, in contrast to complicated problems which can be resolved with structured, methodical plans and specialised knowledge and tools, complex problems demand an adaptive and flexible approach to problem solving (Le Fevre et al., 2019). From their review of research focusing on the change process, Anderson (2009) established that, when change is viewed through a lens of complexity, stages of the change cycle are no longer considered to be linear or sequential. Instead, the stages of the change cycle are seen as interconnected and interdependent, and what happens in one phase will have a direct influence on the events and outcomes of other phases. The greater number of drivers, such as multiple settings or the complexity of systems, makes the change process even less certain because the change process itself is iterative. Each phase informs the change process as it is changing (Fullan, 2020; Le Fevre et al., 2019).

The central role that emotions play in change processes is an example of one such driver that adds to this complexity. Rarely do many leaders consider how teachers will feel or the role that emotions will play as part of the planning for change process and emotions are frequently overlooked in the planning and implementation. Busy leaders often find themselves in the position of making swift assessments and relying on rather haphazard decision-making processes in order to navigate through complex situations (Fullan, 2020; Le Fevre et al., 2019). Yet, emotions affect the ability of individuals to engage in the change process, and as such they can significantly influence the success or failure of any initiative (Le Fevre, 2014; Twyford et al., 2017). Therefore, making time to understand how and why emotions arise as part of the change process and thinking about how to respond appropriately or do things in different ways has the potential to significantly enhance a leader's success in leading change initiatives (Timperley et al., 2020; Twyford & Le Fevre, 2019).

In a world where it is generally seen as up to the individual to manage their own feelings, emotions, and any resulting disengagement from the learning process, emotions can feel untidy or inconvenient in the professional environment (Timperley et al., 2020). Yet, emotions are always present in professional learning and whether we are aware of it or not, our evolving emotional state influences everything we do (Timperley et al., 2020). While it may be tempting to concentrate solely on the structural and operational facets of leadership, the social context and relational-based dimensions of professional learning compel leaders to recognise and address emotions in the context of the change process.

Participating in professional learning involves a process of change that can evoke feelings of excitement, anticipation, and satisfaction. At the same time, change is also inherently risky because it involves uncertainty and feelings of vulnerability, especially in relation to the sense of self and identity (Le Fevre, 2014). Although positive risk-taking is essential for fostering effective innovation, feelings such as fear of change, desire to keep things the same, fear of being judged or criticised, or worry that change may not be possible, all challenge a teacher's sense of professional competency. This aligns with Le Fevre (2014, p. 57), who contends that "expectations to change practice may touch raw nerves because they are likely to impinge on teachers' sense of professional identity and competence". Research by Twyford and Le Fevre (2019) found that the greater the potential for the professional learning process to expose a teacher to feelings of loss of their professional identity, the greater the sense of vulnerability and as such the teacher's perception that the professional learning is inherently risky. Even though teachers may be able to recognise both the positive and negative potential outcomes of professional learning, if they perceive the personal risk associated with the changes being asked of them as too high, they often feel the need to protect their sense of self-identity (Bendikson & Meyer, 2023; Le Fevre, 2014).

Given that the need to replace existing practices with unfamiliar new ones is inherent in strengthening pedagogy, the success of professional learning initiatives hinges on individual teachers actively choosing to engage with and implement proposed changes (Twyford et al., 2017). Disengagement from professional learning initiatives therefore impedes change improvement plans and can disrupt the professional environment. As a result, it can be tempting for leaders to infer that non-engagement or low levels of engagement are an indication of an individual's wilful resistance to do what is needed to make the change happen (Twyford, 2016; Twyford & Le Fevre, 2019).

Research has shown, however, that blaming teacher resistance on the individual in this way is overly simplistic (Twyford & Le Fevre, 2019; Twyford et al., 2017). It ignores the contribution that the context and leaders themselves bring to teachers' experiences of change and the emotional responses that are inherent in the process (Timperley et al., 2020). Indeed, it has been found that, even though teachers may understand and agree with the programme philosophically and have strong motivation to change, they may still exhibit behaviours such as avoidance or non-compliance (Le Fevre, 2014; Twyford et al., 2017). For leaders seeking to engage in sustained cycles of school improvement that result in improved outcomes for learners, it is important, therefore, not to dismiss teacher resistance as simply a lack of willingness to try. Rather, it is vital that leaders work to make sense of the various ways that teachers experience change and help them to engage successfully in the process (Bendikson & Meyer, 2023; Timperley et al., 2020).

Perceptions of risk

Recently, work by Helen Timperley, Deidre Le Fevre, and Kaye Twyford has sought to make sense of emotional responses to change and teachers' engagement in professional learning through the lens of perceptions of risk.

Conceptualising feelings such as uncertainty, resistance, and vulnerability as "risk" is a valuable way for leaders to make sense of and navigate emotions that are inherent to the change process (Bendikson & Meyer, 2023; Twyford et al., 2017). Rather than being physical threats, feelings of risk are mental constructions based on a person's judgement of the uncertainty of current events and future outcomes (Twyford et al., 2017). Perceptions of risk emerge in response to current or expected future events, coupled with feelings of vulnerability regarding potential impacts of those events (Timperley et al., 2020). Feelings of uncertainty about existing capabilities combined with concerns about future capacity to meet the change requirements contribute to a teacher's sense of vulnerability and feelings of risk. The manifestation of perceptions of risk is related to feelings of uncertainty and sense of vulnerability that can come with change because of the inherent problem that we cannot know for sure what the outcome of future events will be.

Perceptions of risk are complex and personal. Perceptions of future uncertainty and levels of risk participants perceive about a programme of change are informed by a wide range of factors, including the individual's prior experiences, beliefs, values, thoughts, and emotions (Twyford et al., 2017). Because levels of perceived risk are influenced by a web of past and current experiences of educational change, the degree to which the sense of risk is felt is different for different people (Le Fevre et al., 2019).

Considering risk this way presents a paradox: while risk is essential for learning and growth, excessive risk can deter willingness to take action (Twyford et al., 2017). Studies of the way perceptions of risk are experienced by teachers engaging in professional learning have found a consistent inverse connection between the presence of risk and willingness to engage in change initiatives (Le Fevre, 2014; Le Fevre et al., 2019; Twyford et al., 2017). Le Fevre et al. explain that "teachers with high perceptions of risk, especially if unrecognized or unacknowledged, are likely to avoid or resist engaging in change" (2019, p. 99).

Examining emotions arising from professional learning through the perspective of perceived risk rather than resistance, allows a leader to shift their attention away from individual teachers and their emotional reactions to the change process. Instead, it reframes the learning process as a journey of risk-taking and directs leaders to understand teachers' experiences amid these challenges (Timperley et al., 2020). For leaders, this means anticipating emotional responses to change and taking steps to minimise perceived risks, reducing uncertainty, and embracing vulnerability as a positive and crucial aspect of the change process. Shifting focus also shifts the responsibility for navigating emotions away from teachers alone. Instead, leaders and teachers are encouraged to work together to create an emotionally supportive environment where it is acceptable for teachers and leaders to show their vulnerability, take risks, and make mistakes (Le Fevre et al., 2019; Timperley et al., 2020).

A framework for navigating emotional responses to change

The framework for navigating perceptions of risk (Table 4.1) presents five interconnecting sets of strategies and actions that leaders can use to help them, and their teachers, navigate the emotions and the sense of vulnerability that are inherent in educational change.

The framework is drawn from a number of New Zealand-based studies and pieces of research about navigating emotional responses to change and perceptions of risk (Le Fevre, 2010, 2014; Timperley, 2011; Twyford, 2016; Twyford & Le Fevre, 2019; Twyford et al., 2017). Ideas from current educational leadership literature relating to leading professional learning have also informed the framework (Bendikson & Meyer, 2023; Le Fevre et al., 2019; Timperley et al., 2020).

Deliberate acts of leadership identified in these works have been synthesised and grouped into two easily accessible themes for leaders to consider: Strengthening knowledge and understanding; and Developing cultures of trust and supportive risk-taking.

These themes and leadership actions are neither linear nor sequential. Instead, they provide a web of connected and interdependent actions that leaders can prioritise prior to and throughout the change process. The themes include both individual and collective actions. Some actions focus on the knowledge and skill-building actions of the leader, others describe actions and engagement that leaders could deploy as part of the professional learning process.

Table 4.1 Framework for navigating perceptions for risk

Theme One: Strengthening knowledge and understanding	
Action One: Build knowledge of change processes Talking more about how the challenges and expectations of change empowers people to understand and engage with the complex and difficult process of making schools more effective for all learners.	
Talk about change processes Feelings of vulnerability and risk can be amplified by lack of clarity about the potential outcomes of the change process. Although it is not always possible to remove all uncertainty in relation to a change initiative, just talking about change processes can build confidence and reduce feelings of vulnerability and risk. This is because pre-emptively talking about risk-taking is an opportunity for leaders to empower teachers to become more metacognitive about predictable emotional responses to change such as feelings of loss or ineffectiveness.	**Leadership action: Systematically talk about change processes** • Embed talk about change processes into everyday leadership actions, not just as part of specific change initiatives. • Involve all stakeholders including educational leaders, professional developers, classroom teachers, and students, where appropriate. • Focus talk about change processes on how participants can anticipate and navigate the complex and difficult process of change.
Create a shared and clear understanding of the purpose and priorities of the change process In complex cycles of iterative school improvement, where the route is more uncertain or where ideal solutions are not readily available, building a shared understanding of the purpose and priorities of the change process reduces uncertainty. Having clarity about the roles and responsibilities of those involved brings a sense of certainty and increases relational trust in the context of an uncertain the change process. This is important because, in the face of an unknowable future, what is not explicitly stated is often interpreted through inaccurate assumptions.	**Leadership action: Talk specifically about the improvement cycle that is being undertaken with specific emphasis on what might happen, what might be expected of participants, and what is yet to be decided on** • Define a clear purpose for the change process from the start. • When it is difficult to describe each step of the change process from the outset, talk instead about the priorities for the change process. • Create clarity about the roles and responsibilities for everyone involved and come back to these at different stages in the process. • Be transparent about the way that change outcomes will be assessed and evaluated.

Action Two: Develop relevant knowledge and skills in others
Effective change processes require participants to step from the known to the unknown. Gaining relevant knowledge and skills reduces uncertainties and introduces new ways of working that boost confidence in taking action.

Prioritise deep learning	Leadership action: Avoid an overload or avalanche of too many change agendas at one time
Feelings of vulnerability are increased when teachers, in the role of learners, doubt whether their knowledge and skills are adequate for the anticipated requirements of the change process. Building their knowledge and capabilities relating to the change initiative in an environment of positive risk-taking reduces teachers' sense of uncertainty as new knowledge underpins increased feelings of confidence.	• Strategically identify change priorities. • Include others in this decision making and share this decision making with others. • Be realistic about the time it takes to embed change initiatives.
	Leadership action: Prioritise deep learning as part of the professional learning process • Seek ways to support teachers to grow their knowledge of what is being asked of them. • Create coherent professional learning plans that ensure enough time for professional learning to be embedded into practice.
Help others to understand the role of emotion in professional learning Considering the widespread presence of emotions in change processes and how feelings like vulnerability can hinder teachers' full engagement, it is beneficial to openly acknowledge how the change process may evoke emotions for participants. This can open conversations and potentially identify commonalities between the concerns of leaders and teachers.	**Leadership action: Promote new learning as potentially uncomfortable** • Acknowledge that emotion is an inevitable part of change and learning and can sometimes be difficult and challenging. • Create systematic opportunities for teachers to discuss their personal experiences of emotions during periods of change. • Share your own experiences of emotions in the learning and change process.

Action Three: Demonstrate knowledge and credibility as a leader

Highly effective educational leaders demonstrate a very specialised knowledge of teaching and learning that in turn makes them effective leaders of learning. They are able to develop relationships built on positive high regard, mutual respect, and relational trust.

Build knowledge of leading processional learning and pedagogical content knowledge A leader's ability to understand, apply, and use specialist knowledge relating to learning and teaching underpins their respectful relationships with their staff because they can conceptualise the work that their teachers are undertaking. Although it is not always reasonable for a leader to understand the subject-specific content knowledge relating to all learning areas in the curriculum, teachers perceive leaders who demonstrate high levels of knowledge about teaching and learning methods and practices as more credible. As such, teachers are more willing to take risks in their own teaching practice or implement suggestions following conversations about professional learning if they consider their leader knowledgeable.	**Leadership action: Prioritise the development of knowledge that is required to effectively lead change processes.** This includes both knowledge and understanding of the underpinning theories related to the professional learning and pedagogical content knowledge about teaching and learning practice **Reflective questions for leaders** • What knowledge and skills do the teachers need for students to meet students' curricula and other goals? • What knowledge and skills do I as a leader need to meet the teachers' learning needs? • What kinds of professional learning do I need to deepen my leadership knowledge and refine my skills? • What do I need to do differently to engage the teachers in new learning experiences? • How will I assess the impact of my changed actions on those outcomes I value? **Leadership action: Engage in the professional learning process alongside staff** • Seek opportunities to work alongside the facilitators who are leading professional learning. This might look like enacting aspects of the leading change process described in this framework. • If you are not taking an active leadership role in the professional learning itself, ensure that you are visible and present throughout the process. • Be a present and active part of professional learning alongside staff.

Theme Two: Developing cultures of trust and supportive risk-taking

Action Four: Foster relational trust

Environments that feature high-quality relationships and supportive cultures impact positively on teachers' abilities to face feelings of vulnerability and take risks.

Anticipate there will be emotional responses, of all degrees and from all involved Given the inevitable nature of emotions in the change process, it is important that leaders acknowledge that there will be feelings of risk in the learning process. Doing so helps a leader to interpret resistance to engage in learning, not as a personal failing on the part of the individual, but as a natural and inevitable part of the change process and react with empathy and effect.	**Leadership action:** Ask questions before and during the change process to build an understanding of how everyone in the change process might feel and experience the learning process **Reflective questions for leaders** • *How might teachers feel about being asked to change their practice?* • *What effect might new learning have on a teacher's sense of themselves as a professional?* • *How risky might teachers perceive different aspects of the professional learning plan to be?* • *What support systems or resources can I put in place to manage and mitigate these risks?* **Leadership action:** Ask questions about your own perceptions of risk **Reflective questions for leaders** • *What potential risks to my sense of self and success do I associate with this change?* • *What information or data do I need to better understand and manage these risks?* • *What might be underpinning my perceptions of risk and uncertainty?* • *How might my past experiences influence how I am thinking about this change process?* • *What support systems or resources do I have in place to manage and mitigate these risks?*

Action Five: Encourage a supportive culture of risk-taking

Teachers, like students, operate within zones of proximal development. They need professional learning environments that provide safe spaces to experiment, fail, and try again.

Foster learning-focused relationships	Leadership action: Show empathy, trust, and respect towards others as you navigate task and relationship demands
Learning-focused relationships celebrate the process as well as the success of outcomes. When relationships focus on learning, they create a culture where participants feel supported to step outside of their comfort zone and take risks without fear that they will be criticised or judged.	• Understand that trust forms through everyday actions and interactions. • Notice what matters and seek to resolve problems that compromise success as they arise. **Leadership action: Know your teachers as learners** • Acknowledge that different professional learning activities are likely to feel riskier for some participants than others. • Seek to understand teachers' reactions to change and collaborate to find ways to engage and support them in taking risks. • Foster the mindset in yourself and others that risk-taking is an essential part of learning.

Continues on next page

Action Five: Encourage a supportive culture of risk-taking

Teachers, like students, operate within zones of proximal development. They need professional learning environments that provide safe spaces to experiment, fail, and try again.

Notice and reduce unnecessary uncertainty Feelings of emotion are inevitable in the change process, and not all feelings of uncertainty can or should be eliminated. Reducing uncertainty where possible provides everyone involved with more capacity to manage the unavoidable emotions. Individuals interpret uncertainty in their own ways, which affects their perceived levels of risk and vulnerability, leading some to perceive more risk than others. Therefore, it is crucial also for leaders to observe and recognise these variations to effectively mitigate uncertainty.	**Leadership action: Identify sources of risk during the development stage of the change process, assess and consider which can be proactively addressed** Reflective questions for leaders • Where is uncertainty likely to occur? • What does it look like? • How do we as leaders contribute to it? • Can we deliberately reduce it? **Leadership action: Develop an understanding of various types of uncertainty to better able to mitigate uncertainty** • Consider different sources of uncertainty such as prior experiences of professional learning, uncertainty about future professional learning events, and uncertainty created by the unknown possible consequences of the future professional learning event. • Acknowledge that some professional learning activities, such as in-class observations, are likely to feel riskier for participants and plan the programme of change and support offered accordingly. **Leadership action: Where perceptions of risk may be unavoidable, provide clear, coherent, and timely detail about aspects of the change process wherever possible**

Conclusion

Leaders who conceptualise learning through a sociocultural lens will intuitively understand the role that building quality relationships—through showing empathy, trust, and respect—has in reducing perceptions of risk and fostering teachers' capacity to engage in cycles of inquiry with more confidence. Designing change initiatives that lead to real and sustained improvements in learner outcomes requires more than just the right dispositions, however. In educational settings with many competing priorities, it is crucial to proactively identify leadership actions that will foster a community of learners equipped with the necessary dispositions and skills to take risks.

For leaders to successfully navigate emotional responses to educational change it is critical that they first grow their own understanding of the way teachers experience feelings of emotion, vulnerability, and risk in relation to professional learning. This increased knowledge will underpin the way leaders are able to make sense of the actions and reactions of their teachers as they engage with change initiatives. It will also lead to deliberate acts of leadership designed to minimise the negative impacts of emotional responses and perceptions of risk.

References

Anderson, S. E. (2009). Moving change: Evolutionary perspectives on educational change. In A. Hargreaves, A. Lieberman, M. Fullan, & D. Hopkins (Eds.), *Second International Handbook of Educational Change* (pp. 65–84). Springer.

Bendikson, L., & Meyer, F. (2023). *It's not rocket science—A guide to the school improvement cycle: With examples from New Zealand and Australian schools* (1st ed.). Myers Education Press.

Fullan, M. (2020). *Leading in a culture of change.* John Wiley & Sons.

Le Fevre, D. (2010). Changing TACK: Talking about change knowledge for professional learning. In H. Timperley & J. Parr (Eds.), *Weaving evidence, inquiry and standards to build better schools* (pp. 71–91). NZCER Press.

Le Fevre, D. (2014). Barriers to implementing pedagogical change: The role of teachers' perceptions of risk. *Teaching and Teacher Education, 38,* 56–64. https://doi.org/10.1016/j.tate.2013.11.007

Le Fevre, D., Timperley, H., Twyford, K., & Ell, F. (2019). *Leading powerful professional learning: Responding to complexity with adaptive expertise.* SAGE Publications.

Timperley, H. (2011). Knowledge and the leadership of learning. *Leadership and Policy in Schools*, *10*(2), 145–170.

Timperley, H., Ell, F., & Le Fevre, D. (2020). *Leading professional learning: Practical strategies for impact in schools*. Australian Council for Educational Research.

Twyford, K. (2016). *Risk or resistance: Understanding teachers' perceptions of risk in professional learning*. [Doctoral thesis, University of Auckland].

Twyford, K., & Le Fevre, D. (2019). Leadership, uncertainty and risk: How leaders influence teachers. *Journal of Professional Capital and Community, 4*(4), 309–324. https://doi.org/10.1108/JPCC-02-2019-0002

Twyford, K., Le Fevre, D., & Timperley, H. (2017). The influence of risk and uncertainty on teachers' responses to professional learning and development. *Journal of Professional Capital and Community, 2*(2), 86–100. https://doi.org/10.1108/JPCC-10-2016-0028

PART 2

LEADERSHIP WITHIN THE EARLY CHILDHOOD SECTOR

Chapter 5

Exploring notions of early childhood leadership in Aotearoa New Zealand

Gwen Davitt and Debbie Ryder

Introduction

The vision of the Teaching Council of Aotearoa New Zealand (previously Education Council New Zealand) is for all teachers to experience the chance to grow their leadership capability and capacity, drawing on the importance of leadership occurring within a collective and relationship-based environment (Education Council New Zealand, 2018). Klevering and McNae (2018) recognise that, whilst there is a plethora of leadership research, there has been limited focus exploring the complexities of leadership specific to the early childhood education (ECE) sector in Aotearoa New Zealand.

This chapter therefore seeks to explore some of the realities of ECE leadership and how an outdated notion of hierarchical leadership no longer reflects the current ECE context or climate. Instead, a new and changing perception of leadership better represents how most ECE teaching teams work and lead. Furthermore, the notion of leadership dispositions is offered as a means of more adequately describing the nature of leadership within an ECE context today. More specifically, leadership dispositions focus on being relationship focused; caring of others; a clear communicator; supportive of the team; a critical friend; and finally, being open to growth and change (Ryder et al., 2017).

With the ever-changing needs of the ECE sector, it is important for teams to view themselves as teacher-leaders. Therefore, in this chapter, a dispositional leadership approach is offered to support leaders to identify and grow not only their own capability, but also the emerging leadership capacity within the teaching team. Three key themes are presented for the reader: realities of ECE leadership; changing the perception of ECE leadership; and a dispositional approach for ECE leadership.

Realities of ECE leadership

In the ECE sector in Aotearoa New Zealand, teachers often find themselves in roles of responsibility without any formal leadership qualifications. Leaders are often learning what it is to be a leader while they are carrying out their role. Weisz-Koves (2011) identified the essential nature of developing teacher leadership in ECE in Aotearoa. Teaching Council of Aotearoa New Zealand reflects this belief in its vision, to "enable every teacher, regardless of their role or setting, to have the opportunity to develop their own leadership capability" (Education Council New Zealand, 2018, p. 4). Yet there is a concern that, overall, ECE teachers do not view themselves as leaders. Whilst effective leadership is a key driver of organisational performance and improvement, Lee et al. (2022) report how leadership has not previously been seen as a lever for quality and improvement within the ECE sector.

The ECE Taskforce (2011) described how leadership in ECE in New Zealand has been traditionally perceived in the form of governance and management. Added to this traditional perspective is a general lack of emphasis on the importance of ECE leadership. Historically, ECE itself has held a low status alongside teaching in the compulsory sector. Due to these factors, there is a progressive lack of strong leadership role models, with teachers experiencing confusion over terminology around leadership and management. Accordingly, the concept of leadership being hierarchical continues to reinforce the perception that ECE leadership is only linked to formal roles (Weisz-Koves, 2011).

Because of these hindering factors, more newly qualified and less experienced teachers are taking on formal leadership positions (Movahedazarhouligh et al., 2022; Weisz-Koves, 2011).

Movahedazarhouligh et al. (2022) argue that a shortage of experienced ECE leaders means there are limited opportunities to "develop the skills and competencies they need to lead in their careers to serve and drive change and improvement in their field communities" (p. 7). The authors explain that specific leadership training is needed to support development of leadership capacity and capability through the "acquisition of knowledge, skills, and dispositions" (Movahedazarhouligh et al., 2022, p. 12) to grow leadership practice. Denee (2018) also emphasises the lack of leadership professional training opportunities which often results in many positional leaders learning on the job or implementing what they believe to be effective leadership in practice without the relevant theoretical underpinnings.

Changing perception of ECE leadership

Lee et al. (2022) discuss how, when ECE teachers understand that leadership is more about a process of working toward change and improvement, and less about a hierarchical approach, they might discover they indeed have a significant role to play. Thus, the perception of ECE leadership requires broadening the view of leadership beyond management functions, to include leadership for change, improvement, and innovation (Lee et al., 2022). To this end, Mackwood (2017) attests to how the experience of being inspired and motivated by a passionate leader encourages one's own aspirations of leadership.

Moreover, Weisz-Koves (2011) refers to teacher leadership as a factor that is directly linked to educational quality (Crowther et al., 2009; ECE Taskforce, 2011; Thornton, 2006; Thornton et al., 2009). Links can be seen to distributed, collaborative, and educational leadership, in which all members of the learning community are encouraged to step up and take responsibility to develop their leadership potential. In this way, leadership opportunities are provided which, in turn, improve teaching and learning outcomes (ECE Taskforce, 2011; Kirby et al., 2021; Thornton, 2006).

Weisz-Koves (2011) focuses on key aspects for change, such as: challenging and transforming deficit perceptions; promoting distributed forms of leadership; fostering teachers' sense of professional efficacy;

and encouraging collaborative leadership. In terms of promoting a distributed approach to leadership, Denee (2018) argues that effective leadership supports collaboration through creation of an open and collegial team environment. It is within this type of environment that robust professional discussion of issues, together with the questioning of current practices, can take place openly (Notman, 2017; Ryder et al., 2017). Extending on these concepts, Denee (2018) explains how teachers who also consider themselves leaders work to inspire, motivate, and lead learning to drive change and continuous improvement.

Turton and Wrightson (2017) describe how they "embrace a collectivist approach favoured by many cultures, where leadership can be demonstrated through leading practices contributed by all members" (p. 22). These authors focus on shared leadership practices that encourage contribution based on an individual's knowledge, skills, and dispositions regardless of whether they are a positional or emergent leader.

A dispositional approach for ECE leadership

In ECE in Aotearoa New Zealand, teachers work in a team context; thus, those in leadership roles are also part of that teaching team. However, leadership in ECE is not only the role of the designated leader. The foundation for effective ECE leadership is underpinned by the development of the leader, as well as that of the teaching team (Deo & Shuchita, 2023). Therefore, this final section talks to six leadership dispositions outlined by Ryder et al. from their 2017 study of ECE leadership. These six dispositions are presented as an approach to building and growing effective leadership through being:

- relationship focused
- caring of others
- a clear communicator
- supportive of the team
- a critical friend
- open to growth and change.

Being relationship focused

One of the key dispositions is that of *being relationship focused*. For leaders to build relational focus within their practice they need to create connections between themselves and the team, and between individual team members (Deo & Shuchita, 2023). Connections build trust, support effective communication, and encourage collegial support (Denee, 2018; Klevering & McNae, 2018) in addition to generating a shared vision (Deo & Shuchita, 2023). It is only when this relational trust is established that a culture of unity and shared purpose can begin to form within the ECE setting (Denee, 2018; Ryder et al., 2017; Education Council New Zealand, 2018).

According to Deo and Shuchita (2023), "building trust, showing respect, and fostering transparency are key elements in forming meaningful relationships and promoting collaboration" (p. 8). Furthermore, relationships need to be reciprocal and culturally responsive (Ministry of Education, 2017; Turton & Wrightson, 2017) to foster leadership potential (Deo & Shuchita, 2023) and to reflect the diverse environments in which leadership is enacted. Reciprocity and responsiveness in leadership need to also value different ways of knowing, being, and doing (Turton & Wrightson, 2017) and thus further nurture ongoing professional relationships.

Being caring of others

Closely connected to being relationship focused is the disposition of *being caring of others*. In fact, one could argue that these two dispositions go together. However, it is important to acknowledge the difference. Being caring starts with believing in the individual teacher, supporting them, and being responsive to enable them to be the best that they can be (Davitt & Ryder, 2018; Williams et al., 2012). Furthermore, by leaders giving and receiving care and respect, Deo and Shuchita (2023) argue that individuals start to see themselves as part of the teaching team and organisation. In this way, leaders are extending and sustaining the essence of care across the leadership practice of individuals and teams (Davitt & Ryder, 2018). By caring for and believing in team members, leaders then believe in themselves and their leadership. Thus, they reciprocate by believing in and caring for others (Mackwood, 2017).

Williams et al. (2012) and Davitt and Ryder (2018) reiterate the importance of leaders being caring and responsive and demonstrating respect and warmth. A teacher in the Ryder et al. (2017) study described gratitude for their leader and how their caring approach builds the teacher's own belief in themselves personally and professionally. Additionally, Deo and Shuchita (2023) also focus on the value of treating others as you expect to be treated; they view this as being foundational to the respectful and nurturing approach of leadership.

Believing in team members provides support and enables leaders to be effective in their practice and leadership (Williams et al., 2012). Deo and Shuchita (2023), also argue for providing nurturing environments that benefit all members of the teaching team and generate positive outcomes for all. Moreover, giving positive feedback to express appreciation of individuals and teams was viewed as a significant way to encourage and nurture a unified team culture (Deo & Shuchita, 2023). In support, Mackwood (2017) describes how receiving appreciation for being open and honest increases one's sense of self, which can then lead to future caring interactions.

Being a clear communicator

The third disposition of an ECE leader is that of *being a clear communicator*. When a leader demonstrates a commitment to open, respectful, and authentic communication, everyone's voice has a chance to be heard (Davitt & Ryder, 2018; Deo & Shuchita, 2023; Ryder et al., 2017; Education Council New Zealand, 2018). Open and honest communication was evident in the Ryder et al. (2017) study, with one leader referring to their communication style as being collegial, collaborative, and robust. The leader's outcome was for the team to move together cohesively, where it was more important for the team to agree to disagree, rather than feeling they needed to seek consensus.

Instead of being necessary to have a congruent communication style where everyone agrees, the emphasis is more on being open to different perspectives (Davitt & Ryder, 2018), and thus to enable effective communication and team unity. This notion of robust communication is further supported by Notman (2017) and Deo and Shuchita (2023) who reiterate how effective communication serves as a tool to enhance team unity. When a team comes together in solidarity through robust communication, it serves to create a shared leadership culture of mutual support and relational trust (Notman, 2017). Modelling clear and supportive communication also reinforces learning about leadership on the job (Notman, 2017). In addition, the Education Council New Zealand (2018) emphasises how open and respectful communication substantiates the critical importance of establishing and sustaining quality professional relationships.

Being supportive of the team

With the first three dispositions in place (i.e., being relationally focused, caring, and a clear communicator), the leader is best placed to turn their attention to building the leadership in others, as evidenced by the fourth disposition, *being supportive of the team*. In being supportive the ECE leader draws on the experience and expertise of the team to develop the emergence of leadership. Glenn (2023) and Denee and Thornton (2017) concur, believing that when those in leadership roles are supportive of their team it allows teachers to grow as emerging leaders. A member of a teaching team in the Ryder et al. (2017) study discussed how their leader created intentional opportunities for team members to have a turn at leading the team. The concept of unity and shared opportunity for leadership links to more commonly understood leadership approaches, such as distributed and shared leadership (Denee & Thornton, 2017).

Robertson (2016) and Bowman (2014) also refer to the importance of leaders being responsive to the potential of others, enabling members of the teaching team to feel motivated and empowered to enact leadership practice. Moreover, Deo and Shuchita (2023) argue that it is critical that those in leadership roles support, encourage, and mentor team members to grow their leadership potential. Klevering and McNae (2018) concur, arguing that it is the role of the leader to unveil the potential in others. Furthermore, Robertson (2016) and Bowman (2014) also support this stance, highlighting the importance of all members of the team being enabled to enact leadership practice, thereby utilising their knowledge and expertise to drive leadership growth, change, and involvement (Lee et al., 2022; Thornton et al., 2009).

Being a critical friend

Now that the leader has established a culture of relational care, sound communication and support for the emergence of leadership, they are able to intentionally provide space for individual leadership growth. Ryder et al. (2017) refer to this as *being a critical friend*. A leader within their study shared how they believed leadership growth will only happen when teachers consider their own resolutions to challenging issues. They believe the more independent the teaching team is with their emergent leadership, the more cohesion will occur overall. Notman (2017) and Klevering and McNae (2018) agree, as they discuss the importance of a symbiotic relationship between leaders and teaching team especially as they traverse the ever-changing ECE climate. The Teaching Council of Aotearoa New Zealand also supports the notion of leaders being responsive to changes in ECE, thus needing to adopt an approach to leadership where they work constructively alongside others (Education Council New Zealand, 2018).

Additionally, Notman (2017) believes in productive working relationships, where leaders need to challenge and be willing to be challenged (Davitt & Ryder, 2018). Similarly, Denee (2018) emphasises the importance of "brave professional dialogue" (p. 71) so that questions can be posed and issues discussed. Klevering and McNae (2018) and Education Council New Zealand (2018) recapitulate that, with the many challenges the ECE sector encounters, it is critically important for teaching teams to share a robust and responsive approach, especially when encountering and navigating change.

Being open to growth and change

With the leader having created a culture that builds leadership within the teaching team, the final disposition promotes *being open to growth and change*. Therefore, it is important for the teaching team to step up into leadership roles to navigate change within the ECE sector. Just as the leader aims to empower the growth in others (Klevering

& McNae, 2018), it is important that the teaching team feels motivated and empowered to enact leadership practice (Bowman, 2014; Robertson, 2016). One leader in the Ryder et al. (2017) study exemplified that knowledge comes from everybody within their team, and the importance of the team sharing their knowledge with each other.

Moreover, Lee et al. (2022) expand on the concept of empowerment to encourage teachers and leaders to utilise their diverse knowledge, expertise, and life experiences to inform and drive growth and change. As Glenn (2023) argues, the importance of drawing on these funds of knowledge and personal life experiences enables team members to share or distribute aspects of the leadership role (Denee & Thornton, 2017). Further Denee (2018) advocates for ensuring that both teachers and leaders have the time, space, and support to engage in professional learning for growth and change.

Conclusion

The chapter commenced by bringing the reader's attention to the work of the Teaching Council of Aotearoa New Zealand, whose aspiration is for all ECE teachers to experience opportunities to grow their leadership capability and capacity (Education Council New Zealand, 2018). As the realities of ECE leadership in Aotearoa New Zealand were unpacked, several factors that hinder all teachers from experiencing leadership opportunities became evident. One of the key hindrances is the more traditional notion of hierarchical leadership. When coupled with the low status ECE can at times hold, the sector is seeing more inexperienced teachers stepping up into leadership roles.

A changing perception of leadership is therefore required—one that more effectively represents how most ECE teaching teams aspire to work and lead alongside each other. As ECE is a collaborative teaching and learning space, in order to see the emergence of leadership from within the setting a unique approach is required. The notion of leadership dispositions was offered as a means of more adequately describing the nature of leadership within the ECE context today. Six leadership dispositions were presented: being relationship focused; caring of others; a clear communicator; supportive of the team; a critical friend; and, finally, being open to growth and change (Ryder et al., 2017).

Through the exploration of notions of ECE leadership within Aotearoa New Zealand, a dispositional framework is provided to support leaders to identify and grow not only their own capability but also the emerging leadership capacity within the teaching team.

References

Bowman, R. F. (2014). Learning leadership skills in elementary school. *Kappa Delta Pi Record, 50*(3), 119–123. https://doi.org/10.1080/00228958.2014.931147

Crowther, F., with Ferguson, M., & Hann, L. (2009). *Developing teacher leaders: How teacher leadership enhances school success* (2nd ed.). Corwin Press.

Davitt, G., & Ryder, D. (2018). Dispositions of a responsible early childhood leader: Voices from the field. *Journal of Educational Leadership, Policy and Practice, 33*(1), 18–31. https://doi.org/10.21307/jelpp-2018-003

Denee, R. (2018). Professional learning and distributed leadership: A symbiotic relationship. *New Zealand Annual Review of Education, 23*, 63–78. https://doi.org/10.26686/nzaroe.v23i0.5284

Denee, R., & Thornton, K. (2017). Effective leadership practices leading to distributed leadership. *Journal of Educational Leadership, Policy and Practice, 32*, 33–45. https://doi.org/10.21307/jelpp-2017-0016

Deo, S., & Shuchita, J. (2023). Building strong connections: The potential of relational leadership to empower early childhood educators as leaders. *He Kupu, 7*(4), 3–10.

ECE Taskforce. (2011). *An agenda for amazing children: Final report of the ECE Taskforce*. Ministry of Education.

Education Council New Zealand. (2018). *The leadership strategy for the teaching profession of Aotearoa New Zealand. Te rautaki kaihautū mō te umanga whakaakoranga o Aotearoa.* https://teachingcouncil.nz/assets/Files/Leadership-Strategy/Leadership_Strategy.pdf

Glenn, K. (2023). The role of self-efficacy. How early childhood leaders can empower collective efficacy. *He Kupu, 7*(4), 25–33.

Kirby, G., Douglass, A., Lyskawa, J., Jones, C., & Malone, L. (2021). *Understanding leadership in early care and education: A literature review*. Office of Planning, Research, and Evaluation, Administration for Children and Families, U.S. Department of Health and Human Services.

Klevering, N., & McNae, R. (2018). Making sense of leadership in early childhood education. Tensions and complexities between concepts and practices. *Journal of Educational Leadership, Policy and Practice, 33*(10), 5–17. https://doi.org/10.21307/jelpp-2018-002

Lee, Y., Douglass, A., Zeng, S., Wiehe Lopes, A., & Reyes, A. (2022). Preparing early educators as frontline leaders and change agents with a leadership development initiative. *International Journal of Childcare and Education Policy, 16*(2), 1–18. https://doi.org/10.1186/s40723-022-00095-z

Mackwood, N. (2017). My authentic journey in leadership. *He Kupu, 5*(1),13–18.

Ministry of Education. (2017). *Te whāriki. He whāriki mātauranga mō ngā mokopuna o Aotearoa—Early childhood curriculum.* https://www.education.govt.nz/assets/Documents/Early-Childhood/ELS-Te-Whariki-Early-Childhood-Curriculum-ENG-Web.pdf

Movahedazarhouligh, S., Banerjee, R., & Luckner, J. (2022). Leadership development and system building in early childhood education and care: Current issues and recommendations. *Early Years. An International Journal of Research and Development, 43*(2), 1–15. https://doi.org/10.1080/09575146.2022.2047899

Notman, R. (2017). Holistic leadership in a high needs early childhood centre. In R. McNae., M. Morrison, & R. Notman (Eds.), *Educational leadership in Aotearoa: Issues of context and social justice* (pp. 130–143). NZCER Press.

Robertson. J. (2016). *Coaching leadership: Building educational leadership capacity through partnership* (2nd ed.). NZCER Press.

Ryder, D., Davitt, G., Higginson, R., Smorti, S., Smith, M., & Carroll-Lind, J. (2017). *Poutoko whakatipu poutoko: Whakamanahia ngā poutoko kōhungahunga hei hautūtanga toitū. Leaders growing leaders: Effective early childhood leaders for sustainable leadership.* Te Rito Maioha Early Childhood New Zealand.

Thornton, K. (2006). Notions of leadership in the New Zealand ECE centres of innovation programme. *New Zealand Annual Review of Education, 15,* 153–167. http://dx.doi.org/10.26686/nzaroe.v0i15.1505

Thornton, K., Wansbrough, D., Clarkin-Phillips, J., Aitken, H., & Tamati, A. (2009). *Conceptualising leadership in early childhood education in Aotearoa New Zealand.* New Zealand Teachers Council. https://hdl.handle.net/10289/5102

Turton, L., & Wrightson, H. (2017). Challenging positional authority: Navigating leadership as collaboration. *He Kupu, 5*(1), 21–27.

Weisz-Koves, T. (2011). Developing teacher leadership in early childhood education in Aotearoa: A potential-based approach. *Journal of Educational Leadership, Policy and Practice, 26*(2), 35–47. doi:10.3316/INFORMIT.805275046795112

Williams, N., Broadley, M. E., & Te-Aho, K. (2012). *Ngā taonga whakaako: Bicultural competence in early childhood education.* Ako Aotearoa National Centre for Tertiary Teaching Excellence.

Chapter 6
Experiences of leading an early childhood education centre during the COVID-19 pandemic

Jo Ellis and Rachel Taylor

Introduction

The COVID-19 pandemic has been described as an unprecedented event in modern history (United Nations, 2020), with significant impacts and ongoing challenges being felt nationally and globally. The uncertainty that came with the pandemic meant that leaders from across different organisations had to adapt their leadership practices to be more task-oriented and responsive to the ever-changing landscape. The event impacted the role of leaders across educational sectors, especially those in the early years sector (Junça-Silva & Caetano, 2024).

In response to the pandemic, on Monday, 23 March 2020, the New Zealand Government announced that Aotearoa New Zealand would be moving to Alert Level 3 and 48 hours later would move to Alert Level 4 to try to stop the transmission of COVID-19 (Gauld, 2023; Kaine et al., 2022). The announcement provided a 2-day transition for early childhood education (ECE) services to prepare their children, families, and staff to move to Alert Level 4. This action caused significant disruption and change in the sector, where leaders were faced with complex and rapid change. This created a sense of disequilibrium and discomfort where leaders had to make sense of the process for themselves. As the literature suggests, the context in which individuals operate can significantly moderate their affective and behavioural reactions to perceived uncertainty (Junça-Silva & Caetano, 2024).

This chapter reports on research focusing on the experiences of four ECE leaders from the Otago region during the COVID-19 pandemic. The emphasis of the research was on how centre leaders navigated the challenges they faced and how this impacted their wellbeing and ability to be effective leaders. Their narratives described strategies they employed to be effective in their leadership roles during the COVID-19 pandemic.

The study

The research conducted was qualitative in nature, as it was believed that this approach would provide detailed insights into the role of a centre leader during the COVID-19 pandemic. This research method enabled the centre leaders to share their experiences, making it a qualitative study. The aim was to generate rich data to develop a better understanding of the challenges faced by centre leaders during the pandemic. Furthermore, the research provided the opportunity to broaden leaders' understanding of the complexities involved in leadership in ECE in New Zealand during the COVID-19 pandemic (Creswell & Poth, 2018; Neubauer et al., 2019). The research question was: "What are the experiences of ECE centre leaders/managers and impacts of the COVID-19 pandemic on their, kaiako, tamariki, and whānau in the Otago region of Aotearoa/New Zealand?".

The researchers had previously conducted an online survey with leaders from ECE centres in the Otago region to understand their experiences during the COVID-19 pandemic. Following this, all participants were invited to attend a focus group to explore the findings in greater depth. Participation in the focus group was voluntary and every measure was taken to ensure confidentiality and the safety of the participants. Three participants attended the focus group face-to-face meeting, and one contributed their ideas at a later date via Zoom. All sessions were recorded for data dissemination and each participant was allocated a Centre Leader number (CLn). The following questions, developed from data generated from the online survey, guided the focus group:

1. What examples can you share with us to support your experiences during COVID-19?

2. What have your challenges been around the vaccine mandate?
3. What are the ongoing challenges?
4. What are you doing to support your wellbeing?

This chapter first describes the impact on the centre leaders' wellbeing and the challenges they faced, including staffing mandates during the COVID-19 pandemic. The chapter then presents five strategies the centre leaders implemented that could be applied during future trauma-related or state-of-emergency events.

Impact on leaders' wellbeing

In their report *Learning in a Covid-19 World*, The Education Review Office (2021) highlighted lessons and successes that ECE could build on in the future. These lessons included leaders' need to look after their wellbeing, establish support networks, and ensure they find a balance between their work and personal lives. Additionally, distributive leadership, whereby both formal and informal leadership practice is shared with others, could well be a useful practice for leaders to relieve pressure and workload (Harris, 2013). Participants in the focus group emphasised that, during the COVID-19 pandemic, the focus on their staff, children, families, and operational aspects dominated their time, work, and energy. This, in turn, impacted their wellbeing. Centre leaders described feeling scared, vulnerable, nervous, and very concerned about what would happen if they got sick. For example, CL1 remembers thinking, "Who's going to do the work? Pay the staff?".

It was evident from the focus group that the centre leaders were in a "reaction" mode of operating during the pandemic. As a result, they did not stop to think about how they could spread their workload. One participant outlined the constant "worry about not keeping up with the information" and feeling they needed to "be available for all stakeholders all the time" (CL1). Adding to this, CL4 stated, "it was so intense and there was no downtime". The vulnerability of the leaders was apparent as they shared their stories, and it became evident during the focus group that their wellbeing had not been a priority for them.

When the focus group was asked about how they supported their wellbeing, their responses were very honest and their vulnerability as leaders became obvious. One leader responded with, "Nothing, but I knew I needed to but there was no time" (CL4). This powerful response demonstrates leaders' fragility and sense of despair regarding the situation they were in. CL1 also commented they did "nothing" to support their wellbeing and "The second day of lockdown was the first time I got a full night's sleep. I was so stressed, I felt protected in my house being at home we knew we'd be okay". CL3 explained during this time they planned how they would exit the ECE sector altogether, "I got my exit strategy underway; it took everything out of me". These findings align with Fullan (2020) who contends that change creates disequilibrium, which can be uncomfortable. Therefore, people must make sense of the process for themselves (Fullan, 2020).

Likewise, in a study of mental health and wellbeing during the pandemic, the relentless pressure was described by a teacher as "My brain feels like a browser with 100 tabs open" (Kim et al., 2022, p. 309). This image resonated with the centre leaders as they discussed the pressure they felt from staff and families to be continuously available and informed about the constantly changing situation.

Challenges of leading during COVID-19

There were multiple challenges involved in leading an ECE centre during COVID-19 including: the volume of ever-evolving information received; lack of support to manage and solve problems insufficient support from governing bodies to solve complex problems; lack of consultation around new policies; and staffing issues.

The volume of ever-evolving information

The volume of information that was continually evolving presented ongoing challenges for the centre leaders. Substantial amounts of information were being "thrown" (CL4) at leaders in response to the pandemic, which impacted their wellbeing and their ability to find effective solutions to respond. Fullan (2020) points out the complexity of big problems such as the pandemic are often rife with dilemmas and contradictions, also reiterating there is not one solution that works for all. However, during the pandemic, centre leaders were expected to have the answers. Centre leaders affirmed that they "felt it was the responsibility of the ECE community to make sense and unpack what was coming at us" (CL1). Centre leaders described the volume of information as relentless and ever-changing, even more so with the conditions of the pandemic (Junça-Silva & Caetano, 2024). CL1 stated, "At times it felt I was responsible for COVID! In the leadership position, people felt that you were the one saying these things".

The Education Review Office (ERO, 2021) acknowledged that the speed at which information was delivered created a challenge for centre leaders. Furthermore, while the Ministry of Education bulletins at the end of each day kept people informed, ERO reported that, for one in 10 leaders, the volume of information presented a challenge. For some centre leaders, this elevated stress levels and added to the relentless pressure they were experiencing. Some changes recommended in the information were left to interpretation. This confused leaders who were trying to make sense of what was required in the everchanging situation (ERO, 2021). Although the Ministry of Education, the Ministry of Health, and other government organisations disseminated information regularly, the leaders felt that "guidelines were way open to interpretation, and this was difficult" (CL3). Several competing operational issues impacted leaders. Some issues that existed before COVID-19 became intensified during the pandemic. For example, centre leaders had to deal with staffing concerns in addition to addressing and implementing new policies and procedures.

At the time I was not the centre manager. I was thrown in the deep end. It was a good learning experience, but it was immense pressure going into different levels, the staffing, whānau needs and my own children had to go to school as well. (CL4)

The focus group further highlighted the constant need to read, create risk assessment plans, forms, and templates and collect COVID-19-related medical data from staff. As one centre leader explained, "it was all foreign to us and I had to step up" (CL4).

Lack of support to manage and solve problems

New policies were developed without any consultation, which the centre leaders found very challenging. Centre leaders had to manage and solve a multitude of interconnected problems, as identified as a challenge by the focus group. Examples of these problems included creating new policies, cleaning schedules, and adhering to new guidelines recommended by the Ministry of Education and the Ministry of Health. Leaders were submerged in often unhelpful and distracting information. They had to decipher and interpret information quickly. This meant they were forced to make decisions and act at a faster pace (Fullan, 2020). CL4 stated: "In terms of the MoE and ERO it actually felt like they were more productive. They kept throwing things at us. It was a lot, layer upon layer with financial implications".

Staffing issues

The centre leaders identified that before COVID-19 the Otago region had already faced staffing issues including attracting qualified staff. This challenge was exacerbated during the pandemic once mandated vaccinations for ECE staff were introduced. Staff shortages continued to put pressure on centre leaders as they were unable to fill fixed-term contracts, let alone permanent ones. "I lead a small community-based centre. I was teaching then having to work through employment processes when staff chose not to vaccinate" (CL2). The vaccine mandates placed further strain on the centre leaders as some staff were undecided on whether to get the vaccine.

Evidence suggests that staff were faced with an ethical dilemma around choosing to be vaccinated or risk losing their employment, and that this caused some divide in the education sectors (Teschers et al., 2021). "It was horrible having to let teachers go because they had not been vaccinated" (CL1). Centre leaders felt blamed for following legislation that resulted in having to let staff go. This was a new reality for centre leaders who did not have the human resources experience to manage these situations. CL2 explained they "had to pay for human resources advice to support our parent centre committee".

The COVID-19 pandemic highlighted other unique challenges for leaders, including providing an equitable workplace, working from home, transitioning to distance teaching and, in some cases, staff teaching their own children. An additional challenge was staff absenteeism upon the return to the ECE setting as COVID-19 numbers rose in the community. The staff, their families, and close contacts were required to isolate, sometimes for more than the required 14-day period.

The centre leaders in the focus group explained that they felt compromised in their understanding of "what defines an essential worker" (CL1). They felt that definitions were vague and so centre leaders needed to make their own ethical decisions around this. These differed between leaders which created stress and uncertainty. They described the huge pushback they felt from staff who were defined as an essential worker, including parents, as this impacted on the availability of spaces for children at the centre. At the beginning of the COVID-19 pandemic, a definition of an essential worker was published in national and local newspapers as "any person employed or contracted as a doctor, nurse, midwife, pharmacist, paramedic, medical laboratory scientist, kaiāwhina worker, social worker, aged care and community worker, and caregiver more generally" (Goatley et al., 2020, para. 8).

These experiences were felt much more widely than the four CLs in the focus group. As the ERO report highlighted, around one in three leaders said that their kaiako were experiencing anxiety. This was most commonly related to the uncertainty created by the changing COVID-19 situation, but also referred to job security and added worry for those people who were considered medically vulnerable. (ERO, 2021, p. 18)

Strategies to effectively lead an ECE centre through COVID-19

This section highlights five strategies that arose within the focus group discussion as effective ways of leading an ECE centre through challenging times. In alignment with Fullan (2020), it was evident the centre leaders were committed and not willing to give up positive teaching and learning environments.

1. Seek support from others

It was important to the leaders that they sought support from each other as they navigated how to be effective leaders during a pandemic. Junça-Silva and Caetano (2024) highlighted that effective leadership requires leaders to mitigate perceived uncertainty where possible. Networking became an important tool for supporting each other. The Education Review Office (2021) also reported stand-alone ECE services establishing their support networks as a strategy for making sense of the volume of information that was being sent, notably from the Ministry of Education and the Ministry of Health. Those centre leaders in the focus group who were part of a larger organisation were often able to seek support from their senior managers, who provided reassurance and clarification about what was required of them to correctly respond to the evolving advice set out by the government.

Support from other centre leaders was beneficial, some explained how they met regularly to connect with other centre leaders to help work through problems. As CL3 explained, "What helped me most was the Zoom meetings, offloading, it was confidential, and we cared about each other, we all had the same issues and we learnt from each other". The centre leaders felt supported by having "hui with a wine or a coffee to discuss and share" (CL1).

2. Provide clear and regular communication

Leaders need to demonstrate clear, consistent, and regular communication, particularly during events such as a pandemic. This communication was shown to be important when updating families on additional health and safety requirements that were implemented during the pandemic (ERO, 2021). The emotional wellbeing of staff and families was a major concern for the centre leaders. One centre leader noted that "we were worried about domestic violence, family stress" (CL1). Therefore, it was important that the ECE setting kept in contact with families to let them know they were not alone, and that the setting was there to support them in any way they could. Leaders reported that using digital technology to regularly communicate with children and families meant that "kaiako (teachers) were an ongoing part of children's daily lives" (ERO, 2021, p. 14).

Phone calls, emails, Zoom meetings, and videos posted on Storypark and Educa (online recording sites) were useful strategies for ensuring leaders and staff could remain connected with the families and children. Together, many staff and families established a pattern of engagement that was both supportive and responsive. Effective leadership during uncertain times can provide certainty, clarity, and transparency which creates a climate of trust within the team. Clear communication empowers others and demonstrates effective leadership. It is therefore a crucial strategy to alleviate some of the pressure that comes with being a leader during traumatic events (Junça-Silva & Caetano, 2024).

3. Adapt approaches to teaching and learning

Fullan (2020) discusses how difficult leadership is in a challenging climate. However, once people start to make meaning of the change, it may be perceived positively. In accordance with this, the centre leaders discussed how they felt very proud of how their staff were coping and how they adapted to working from home. Staff had to adjust their view of teaching and implement new strategies for teaching from home. New skills were identified as staff learnt how to make videos for children and how to make video calls via Zoom. Alongside this, it was important to the centre leaders that they provided a purpose for their staff's days, they did this by being "clear about our expectations of working from home. Our teachers did some amazing things" (CL1). The participants in the focus group discussed how proud they were of their teams and their teams' ability to adapt quickly to the complex conditions that the pandemic presented.

4. Empower staff, delegate, and distribute leadership responsibilities

The centre leaders discussed the importance of balancing workloads and making it fair for everyone during lockdown. Leaders employed strategies such as giving staff responsibilities, delegating tasks, helping create new policies, and being part of sub-committees for health and safety and curriculum focus groups.

It could be argued that the adaptive resilience shown by staff reflected the effective leadership demonstrated and role modelled to them by their centre leaders. It has been suggested that solutions to problems may come from the people closest to the situation. Effective leaders who implement leadership strategies empower people to tackle tough problems collectively (Fullan, 2020). Regular team leader meetings provided opportunities to empower staff and allowed them to be part of creating solutions on how to implement new procedures into their daily teaching practice. Centre leaders discussed how this empowered staff: "Our staff felt they had a sense of control of something" (CL3).

Harris (2013, p. 548) states that "distributed leadership encompasses both formal and the informal forms of leadership practice within its framing, analysis and interpretation". Therefore, this leadership style could have been useful to employ in this situation because the positional leaders could have relieved some of their pressure by working collaboratively with their teams.

The centre leaders discussed how they developed strategies where they "tried to lift the information away from them personally and explain to their staff that specific information had come from the mandate or the bulletin etc." (CL1). This was a useful strategy implemented by leaders to effectively explain how decisions made were often out of their control.

Some centre leaders demonstrated distributed leadership where all members of staff were encouraged to take personal and group responsibility. This strategy can be used to develop the staff's leadership potential to improve teaching and learning outcomes and the centre culture (Weisz-Koves, 2011). Centre leaders tried to encourage collaboration and build positive teaching and learning cultures, although at times this process was difficult and complex. Weisz-Koves (2011) highlights the importance of mutual trust, role modelling, power sharing, and democratic processes during times of fear, anxiety, and the unknown. Centre leaders understood the need to redefine new and different working relationships with their staff and families.

5. Prioritise wellbeing

Many leaders took on additional work, responsibilities, and roles as they supported children and their families during and after lockdown. These efforts took a toll on their wellbeing. Centre leaders used a variety of strategies to support and prioritise their wellbeing, such as going fishing, walking, spending time alone, using support services such as the Employee Assistance Program (EAP), and, most importantly, learning alongside others. The centre leaders discussed "doing proactive work that made me feel better" (CL1). Moving forward, ensuring the wellbeing of ECE leaders has been identified by ERO as being critical (ERO, 2021).

Conclusion

There is no doubt that ECE centre leaders were confronted with complex and multiple challenges during the COVID-19 pandemic. The centre leaders who participated in the research shared personal and professional insights regarding the event's impact on their ability to lead their teams and communities effectively. Their experiences highlighted the role of a leader during this time as being intense, relentless, and invariably impacting on their wellbeing. In addition, their knowledge of the direct impact they had on their teams and communities added extra stress as their responsibilities and roles were increased during this time.

This chapter presents five strategies the centre leaders employed, including: support from others; supporting families and open communication; approaches to learning and teamwork; empowering staff, delegating and distributed leadership; and finally, looking after their wellbeing. These strategies ensured challenges that emerged were successfully managed and supported effective leadership of their ECE centre through COVID-19. While these strategies relate to leadership within the ECE sector, they are transferrable and could be useful for leaders in other sectors during future trauma-related or state-of-emergency events.

References

Creswell, J., & Poth, C. (2018). *Qualitative inquiry and research design: Choosing among five approaches* (4th ed.). SAGE Publications.

Education Review Office [ERO]. (2021). *Learning in a Covid-19 world: The impact of Covid-19 on early childhood education* (pp. 1–30). Te Ihuwaka—Education Evaluation Centre. https://ero.govt.nz/our-research/learning-in-a-covid-19-world-the-impact-of-covid-19-on-early-childhood-education

Fullan, M. (2020). *Leading in a culture of change* (2nd ed.). John Wiley & Sons.

Gauld, R. (2023). A review of public policies on Covid-19: The New Zealand experience. *Public Administration and Policy: An Asia–Pacific Journal, 26*(1), 10–20. https://doi.org/10.1108/PAP-04-2022-0028

Goatley, T., Wilson, K., & Brougham, S. (2020, March 25). *COVID-19 Are you an essential service?* Bell Gully. https://www.bellgully.com/insights/covid-19-are-you-an-essential-service/

Harris, A. (2013). Distributed leadership: Friend or foe? *Educational Management & Administration Leadership, 41*(5), 545–554. https://doi.org/10.1177/1741143213497635

Junça-Silva, A., & Caetano, A. (2024). Uncertainty's impact on adaptive performance in the post-COVID era: The moderating role of perceived leader's effectiveness. *Business Research Quarterly, 27*(1), 40–56. https://doi.org/10.1177/23409444231202809

Kaine, G., Greenhalgh, S., & Wright, V. (2022). Compliance with Covid-19 measures: Evidence from New Zealand. *PLoS ONE, 17*(2): e0263376. https://doi.org/10.1371/journal.pone.0263376

Kim, L. E., Oxley, L., & Asbury, K. (2022). "My brain feels like a browser with 100 tabs open": A longitudinal study of teachers' mental health and well-being during the COVID-19 pandemic. *British Journal of Educational Psychology, 92*(1), 299–318. https://doi.org/10.1111/bjep.12450

Neubauer, B. E., Witkop, C. T., & Varpio, L. (2019). How phenomenology can help us learn from the experiences of others. *Perspectives on Medical Education, 8*, 90–97. https://doi.org/10.1007/s40037-019-0509-2

Teschers, C., Devine, N., & Couch, D. (2021). Editorial: Ethics and teacher vaccinations during COVID-19. *Teacher's Work, 18*(2), 52–57. https://doi.org/10.24135/teacherswork.v18i2.337

United Nations. (2020). *The virus that shut down the world: 2020, a year like no other.* UN News Global Perspective Human Stories. https://news.un.org/en/story/2020/12/1080702

Weisz-Koves, T. (2011). Developing teacher leadership in early childhood education in Aotearoa through a potential-based approach. *Journal of Educational Leadership, Policy and Practice, 26*(2), 35–47. https://search.informit.org/doi/abs/10.3316/informit.805275046795112

Chapter 7

Professional learning to support effective leadership in early childhood education

Penny Smith and Monica Cameron

Introduction

Over the past 20 years or so, leaders in Aotearoa New Zealand early childhood education (ECE) settings have had to adapt their leadership practices in response to an ever-changing sector. The contested nature of the sector has seen it vulnerable to the whims of the Government of the day and this has resulted in challenges around funding, ratios, and staffing (Mitchell, 2019). In addition, demand for longer opening hours and increasing numbers of tamariki with diverse needs creates complex challenges for those in leadership roles in the early childhood sector. Being able to adapt and respond to a continually changing education landscape requires leadership practices that intuitively understand and support the needs of the local community, whilst balancing the requirements of regulatory bodies (Mitchell, 2012). Leading effectively through change processes is important, demanding work for ECE leaders.

It is known that effective leadership has a tangible impact on the experiences of kaiako and tamariki, and therefore has the potential to lift the quality of the sector (Cooper, 2019). However, for this to occur, it is essential for early childhood leaders to have a deep understanding of the skills, personal attributes, and knowledge to lead kaiako within their teams to ensure all tamariki and whānau experience high-quality teaching and learning.

Preparing for leadership roles has, for a large part, been ad hoc, whereby most leaders have learnt about the role through observing and pitching in (Rogoff, 2014). For others, learning about leadership has occurred after being appointed to a leadership position. While there are likely many positive opportunities to learn about leadership in these ways, there are also potential challenges. An example of this is when leaders have not experienced positive role models. In this situation, they may be unlikely to have the skills and knowledge required to effectively lead. Additionally, without positive role modelling, leaders may replicate the less effective leadership approaches they may have been exposed to, potentially engaging in dysfunctional communities of practice (Mládková, 2015). It is important to note that those already in leadership roles may also feel that they do not have the support and knowledge they need to be effective, despite already holding positional responsibilities.

While the literature outlines the importance of effective leadership, there appear to be significant gaps in the preparation of, and support for, both leaders and aspiring leaders here in Aotearoa New Zealand (Cooper, 2019; Thornton, 2019). Although there are resources available to support leaders and aspiring leaders, such as the *Educational Leadership Capability Framework* (*ELCF*) (Education Council, 2018), opportunities for leaders and aspiring leaders to learn about the theory and research that underpin effective leadership practices are limited. This chapter focuses on a postgraduate programme designed specifically to bridge this gap in support for those in leadership roles, or aspiring leaders, by providing participants with opportunities to learn about effective leadership in early childhood settings.

Effective leadership

Effective leadership requires leaders to enact a range of leadership practices to influence both current and future development and growth of both ECE settings and the people within them. According to the Education Council New Zealand (2018):

> Leadership in educational organisations in Aotearoa New Zealand is essentially influencing others to act, think, or feel in ways that

advance the values, vision and goals of the organisation, and the learning and flourishing of each of its learners. Leadership is also about seeking sustainable and ongoing improvement and innovation. It is visible in a range of purposeful actions and ways of working. (p. 3)

The current leadership focus in the ECE sector is on enacting effective leadership practices that align with the collaborative nature of the sector, and particularly the use of distributed models of leadership. A distributed approach to leadership is one whereby roles and responsibilities are shared amongst team members based upon their strengths, skills, and interests (Denee & Thornton, 2021; Heikka et al., 2021; Thornton et al., 2009).

The study

This chapter is informed by a study that explored the experiences of a postgraduate leadership programme offered by an initial teacher education provider in Aotearoa New Zealand. Throughout the programme, students engage with each other, as well as the course content, in an online community of practice. The programme content covers a range of leadership-focused aspects, including leadership from a range of cultural perspectives, as well as theories and models of leadership. The programme focused on in the study is an applied practice programme and attracts enrolments from kaiako working across a range of different types of ECE services and a range of roles, including positional leaders and aspiring leaders. The programme is underpinned by kaupapa Māori concepts, specifically identity, and provides the opportunity for students to focus on leadership through both Pasifika and Māori lenses.

An invitation to participate in an online survey was sent to all graduates of the programme prior to 2022, with 31 responses being gathered. Most of the participants had completed their initial teacher education qualification on average 12 years before completing the programme. The participants had between 2 and 36 years of teaching experience in the ECE sector, with the average length of service being 12 years. The survey respondents, for the most part, were working in the ECE sector and therefore experiencing leadership within the sector currently and engaging in leadership practices on a day-to-day basis. The programme aims to be a positive influence on the ECE sector in relation to leadership, by supporting the leadership identity of and development of its graduates.

This chapter shares the perspectives of participants, while connecting to the extant literature. Findings related to the skills, personal attributes, and knowledge the participants identified as being critical to effective leadership in ECE are initially outlined and discussed. This is followed by an exploration of the impacts of the programme on leadership and the opportunities for implementing leadership.

Findings: Critical aspects of effective leadership

When asked about what they believed were the most important aspects of effective leadership, the participants identified skills, personal attributes, and knowledge. The skills identified were focused on interpersonal competences that supported leaders to engage with others. Alongside these came personal attributes that the participants recognised as being critical to effective leadership and aspects of leadership knowledge. The participants' own learning in relation to skills, knowledge, and attributes will now be explored in more detail.

Skills

The participants noted the need for leaders to have a range of interpersonal skills that supported them to engage with others. Skills such as being able to have challenging conversations, which involve both listening and diplomacy, were specifically noted. The ability to be empathetic and understand situations and perspectives was identified as being an important skill for leaders to possess. Being able to work collaboratively with others, engaging in a community of practice (Wenger, 2000) to support team learning, and operating as a team player while also inspiring team members to develop and evolve as teachers, were also viewed as being important. Communication skills were the most commonly mentioned skills across the data, with significant emphasis on the need for leaders to have strong verbal and written communication skills. Communication was seen as being central to effective leadership, including communication within and across teams, but also with families and others who engage with the ECE setting (Seve-Williams, 2017). The following response is reflective of this:

> That leadership involves A LOT of communication, and aroha. That the adults you are working with kind of take the place of the tamariki you used to spend all your time thinking about—that now, it's the team members who you are teaching, guiding, caring for, and nurturing ... (Participant 1)

Reflection, and the ability to critically self-reflect on their own interactions as a leader, was seen as being an important skill, with the importance of leaders to engage in and lead reflection being supported by Stamopoulos and Barblett (2018). This is further supported by Marnell and Thornton (2021), who also draw attention to reflective thinking if there are to be changes in teaching practice. The ability to engage in and lead change requires a growth mindset so leaders critically reflect on what is happening already, including ways that practice and leadership can be developed and strengthened.

Personal attributes

Participants in the study emphasised the importance of possessing a range of personal attributes to support effective leadership. Communication, including the ability to actively listen to views being shared by others, was a key theme amongst the survey responses. The development of interpersonal skills, including empathy, was also noted, with participants talking about the value of leaders being able to engage with and relate to others. For example, Participant 14 noted that it was important to:

> Be open-minded and open-hearted, [an ability] to inspire teams and instill a growth mindset, and be able to remain professional and confidential. I think it's also important that leaders are able to know

their teachers, their quirks, their strengths and weaknesses as well as nurture their wellbeing.

Of note, a number of these personal attributes were also acknowledged by participants as being important skills for leaders to possess and demonstrate, highlighting the connected nature of both skills and personal attributes. Furthermore, the need for leaders to be self-aware and demonstrate their own commitment to learning was also evident. This was important because leaders supported change, growth, and development of team members; the ongoing development of teaching practice; and the vision of the setting. For example, Participant 28 noticed the importance of having an "open mind to listen to other perspectives [with a] love of learning to remain 'current' within the sector; [an] inclusive approach to leadership, celebrating and encouraging everyone's strengths". It is worth noting, however, that an emphasis on personal traits is associated with earlier leadership theories (Stamopoulos & Barblett, 2018) that promote ideas about some people being "born leaders" because they have particular personal traits.

Knowledge

When outlining the knowledge that participants believe leaders need to have as they take on leadership positions, several themes were evident. Participants highlighted the importance of knowing effective strategies for dealing with individuals within teams, including the need to contend with and harness conflict positively as a tool for fostering connection and growth. As part of supporting individuals within a team, participants noted the need for leaders to be cognisant about the ways individual people learn, whilst also being knowledgeable about how to provide pastoral care and support. Leaders having knowledge of individual members of the team, and how to effectively lead all team members, was also noted by participants and supported by Gibbs (2020). Participants, again supported by Gibbs, emphasised the need for leaders to have strong pedagogical knowledge themselves, so as to be able to role model and mentor team members.

Participants suggested that understanding the theories behind leadership styles constituted part of the knowledge base that leaders need, as is supported by Cooper (2014) and Stamopoulos and Barblett (2018). In addition, the importance of being able to access, understand, and apply current knowledge and research related to effective leadership was also identified by participants. As noted by Participant 25: "I believe it's important for leaders to know what type of leader they are and the research and theory behind it". Participants' knowledge of the operational aspects of managing an early childhood service was also highlighted. This included knowledge related to regulatory, health and safety, and legislative requirements, as well as understanding the role of the Ministry of Education and the Education Review Office in Aotearoa New Zealand. Furthermore, the need to understand the difference between leadership and management was noted, though the points around regulatory requirements, etc. in fact relate to management rather than leadership, showing the potential overlap between these terms.

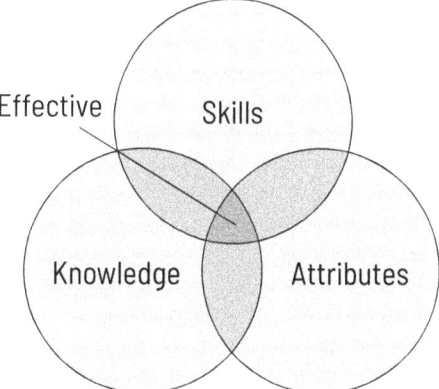

Figure 7.1 Effective leadership

As shown in this section, and in Figure 7.1, the participants in the study clearly signalled that leaders require particular skills, personal attributes, and knowledge to effectively undertake their role. The combination of these factors appears to be key to implementing effective leadership in ECE settings.

Impact of engaging in the programme

Almost all participants indicated that their leadership knowledge was enhanced because of engaging in the programme of study. Aspects of knowledge that were particularly evident included leadership styles, where participants became cognisant of different ways of approaching and applying leadership. Additionally, participants reported learning about how to be effective leaders of change management, enabling them to lead teams through change, so that teachers could be positive change agents to support quality improvement (Cooper, 2014). Developing knowledge around coaching and/or mentoring, such as strategies for supporting the development of the team and team members' own leadership capabilities, was highlighted. Statements such as in the following quote highlight the knowledge development that was supported through engagement in the programme:

> I learnt about the type of leader I am and how it translates into my practice as a teacher and leader. I also learnt about challenges that ECE are facing and how as a leader I contribute [to] this. I learnt more about facilitating leadership opportunities for emerging leaders. (Participant 25)

Engaging in the programme also supported participants to think about the bigger picture, both of education and ECE, so that they were able to engage in strategic thinking and strategic leadership. Through such thinking, participants were also better able to see their role as transformative leaders, both in terms of fostering growth within their teams and also in nurturing positive change within the sector. For example, a participant noted that leaders' influence is widespread, stating that:

> So much—tactfulness, different types of leadership and when to use it, pedagogical content, so many theories and researchers' perspectives. Knowing it [leadership] is not a one-stop 'system' but an evolving, developing, and changing way of being depending on what is coming to you at the moment. (Participant 19)

This quote provides evidence of the ways in which the *ELCF* and, in particular, the strategic thinking and planning capability within the framework, are being used to grow participant knowledge of leadership. The *ELCF* is a core document within the programme and is used to support students to develop their knowledge and understanding of effective leadership.

When asked how their engagement in the programme changed their leadership practice, it was very clear that the programme supported participants to grow their confidence in their own leadership practices as they engaged with their communities of practice (Wenger, 2000; Wenger & Snyder, 2000). Participants gave examples of how their learning had impacted on their own practice, and on the teaching practices of those who they were leading. The growth in confidence reported by participants suggests that the programme affirmed their leadership practices, and that the learning validated their existing skills, knowledge, and attributes. The programme also provided an impetus to add to existing funds of knowledge and created opportunities for participants to try new ways of leading based on the extant research and literature. Participant 3 noted, "I learnt about the complexity of why some things have worked for me and other things not. It gave me confidence to take on a new and big challenge after 15 years at the same centre".

A further impact of the programme for the participants was the disruption of existing knowledge and practices relating to their leadership practice. Participants talked about how the learning they had engaged in had challenged their thinking about how they currently led their team and the programme had in fact been transformative for some of the participants. They provided examples of shifts in practice as a result of engagement, such as:

> Before embarking on my leadership journey, there were a few occasions where I walked past things because it was too hard to address. By gaining more confidence to address situations at the time (within reason), I am able to empower kaiako to provide a high-quality curriculum ensuring best practice is the top priority. It was through the engagement in the programme and course readings that gave me the knowledge and further developed my skills as a leader. (Participant 9)

As noted earlier, the connections to the *ELCF* inherent within the programme supported of participants not only learning about aspects of leadership but of moving to implement what they learnt in ways that supported transformative practice and making the changes that are needed at all levels of the ECE system (Cooper, 2019). A strong example of this was provided by one of the participants who noted that their learning led them to establish an "Aspiring Leaders" programme within their organisation as a way of supporting emergent leaders to help ensure future leaders were well supported. Such experiences led to the "realisation that leadership programmes and role models are so lacking in ECE, [so I] was able to do something about this with [the] establishment of [an] Aspiring Leaders programme where I work" (Participant 4).

An initiative such as the "Aspiring Leaders" programme not only supports those involved, but also helps to ensure sustainability of leadership through succession planning, again linking to the *ECLF*. Engagement in the programme impacted on how the participants went about the day-to-day practice of leadership and to see leadership potential within members of their team. They were able to support the development of other leaders and aspiring leaders within their teams. Moving to more distributed leadership practices (Denee & Thornton, 2021) as a result of learning in the programme was also evident; affirming for them the value of distributed approaches to leadership.

When describing how their participation in the programme impacted on their leadership practice, participants noted their increased confidence, and ability to "hold their own":

> Where do I begin. The short answer is everything that I know about being an effective leader, organisational structures, creating cohesive teams, making space [for] others to grow their leadership skills, sharing the load (distributed leadership) and acknowledging my own bias and accepting other points of view. (Participant 6)

Thematic data analysis has revealed the positive impact of the programme across a number of different aspects of effective leadership knowledge, which has in turn supported participants to implement their learning and to in turn transform their leadership practices.

Opportunities for implementing leadership

In reporting on the opportunities that arose from their engagement in the programme, it was clear that several participants moved into positional leadership roles either during or following the completion of the programme. Engaging with the programme empowered the participants as leaders, whereby some were more able to see themselves as leaders and to also seek out other leadership roles and opportunities. The programme itself added to the participants' knowledge base, as well as providing impetus to seek out leadership roles as they learnt about the leadership possibilities within and outside of the ECE sector. It was also clear that engagement in the programme supported the participants to increase their confidence in their own knowledge and abilities, thereby supporting them to apply for other roles. For example, at the time of starting this qualification, 12 participants were employed in teaching roles compared with six at the time of completing this survey, because they had moved into leadership roles, while six remained in teaching roles. This was specifically noted by Participant 1, who stated that "It also meant that I left that job to lead a brand-new centre where I had a hand in establishing the culture and curriculum".

Furthermore, four had gained positions in tertiary education roles following completion of the qualification, while none were in tertiary education roles prior to enrolling in the programme. While it cannot be assumed that completion of the programme was the only factor influencing their move into these types of leadership roles, given the number who had moved into tertiary education it is likely. The completion of postgraduate-level qualifications is often a requirement for working in tertiary education, and the programme clearly provides a pathway to these qualifications.

The programme supported participants in developing their knowledge of the leadership-focused research and literature, which in turn provided opportunities for self-reflection and growth, such as was articulated here:

> Leadership identity is always changing so self-awareness, self-growth and change are your friends. In learning all about different styles of

leadership I was able to reflect on my own practices. This was both reaffirming and challenging. It gave me reasoning and purpose behind my actions and encouraged me to try out new strategies. (Participant 21)

The quote above provides evidence of the transformative nature of the programme. Engaging in learning about leadership promotes opportunities for both understanding of yourself as a leader and for critical reflection on your leadership practice. The importance of self-reflection has been noted by Marnell and Thornton (2021), who emphasise how this process underpins changes in teacher and leader practice. In learning about leadership theories and approaches, participants were supported to not only identify what they were currently doing and to put this knowledge into practice, but also to also consider other approaches that might be beneficial to their leadership practice and development. Again, participants' engagement in the programme impacted positively on the leadership opportunities that subsequently arose, and that participants now saw themselves as leaders and therefore put themselves forward for positional leadership roles.

Conclusion

In conclusion, the participants in this study identified a range of skills, personal attributes, and knowledge that they believed were significant for leaders to know and use in their leadership practices, as was demonstrated in Figure 7.1. The programme outlined here provided opportunities for the participants to delve deeply into leadership and its many facets through engagement in course work, reading, and participating in an online community of practice. As the results of the study reported in this chapter highlight, having focused opportunity to learn about and to implement effective leadership is instrumental in supporting the growth of leaders. The ripple effects of this programme were clearly evident from the research findings, and the programme is supporting quality leadership in practice. Being part of a learning community focused on leadership learning and development was found to be affirming, and exposed participants to different perspectives. Participants acknowledged the opportunities to learn from each other, to learn from the extant research and literature, and to put this knowledge into practice to support shifts in their leadership practices.

The findings of this study highlight the importance of skills, personal attributes, and knowledge that are critical within the leader's role. Engaging in communities of practice, such as the online community that participants in this programme are part of, supports the development of the skills, personal attributes, and knowledge underpinning effective leadership. Participants' engagement in this programme has the potential to support enhanced leadership practices across a sector that has had few leadership-focused learning opportunities in the past. The development of effective leaders within the ECE sector is critical given the range and pace of change the sector is experiencing. Leaders who are knowledgeable and skillful can support positive change in and across the sector.

References

Cooper, M. (2014). 'Everyday teacher leadership': A reconceptualization for early childhood education. *Journal of Educational Leadership, Policy and Practice, 29*(2), 84–96.

Cooper, M. (2019). Sooner, rather than later. Addressing leadership development in ECE—A response to the *Strategic Plan for Early Learning 2019-29. Early Childhood Folio, 23*(1), 33–36. https://doi.org/10.18296/ecf.0061

Denee, R., & Thornton, K. (2021). Distributed leadership in ECE: Perceptions and practices. *Early Years. An International Research Journal, 41*(2–3), 128–143. https://doi.org/10.1080/09575146.2018.1539702

Education Council New Zealand. (2018). *Educational Leadership Capability Framework.* https://teachingcouncil.nz/assets/Files/Leadership-Strategy/Leadership_Capability_Framework.pdf

Gibbs, L. (2020). Leadership emergence and development: Organizations shaping leading in early childhood education. *Educational Management, Administration and Leadership,* 1–22. https://doi.org/10.1177/1741143220940324

Heikka, J., Pitkäniemi, H., Kettukangas, T., & Hyttinen, T. (2021). Distributed pedagogical leadership and teacher leadership in early childhood education contexts. *International Journal of Leadership in Education, 24*(3), 333–348. https://doi.org/10.1080/13603124.2019.1623923

Marnell, C. E., & Thornton, K. (2021). Leadership practices and indicators of quality, connected through internal evaluation processes in the New Zealand ECE sector.

New Zealand Annual Review of Education, 27, 60–78. https://doi.org/10.26686/nzaroe.v27.8032

Mitchell, L. (2012). Markets and childcare provision in New Zealand: Towards a fairer alternative. In E. Lloyd & H. Penn (Eds.), *Childcare markets. Can they deliver an equitable service?* (pp. 97–113). Policy Press.

Mitchell, L. (2019). Turning the tide on private profit-focused provision in early childhood education. *New Zealand Annual Review of Education, 24*, 75–89. https://doi.org/10.26686/nzaroe.v24i0.6330

Mládková, L. (2015). Dysfunctional communities of practice—Thread for organization. *Procedia—Social and Behavioural Sciences, 210*, 440–448.

Rogoff, B. (2014). Learning by observing and pitching in to family and community endeavours. *Human Development, 57*(2/3), 69–81. https://www.jstor.org/stable/26764709

Seve-Williams, N. (2017). ECE leadership in our times. *He Kupu—The Word, 5*(1), 1–2.

Stamopoulos, E., & Barblett, L. (2018). *Early childhood leadership in action. Evidence-based approaches for effective practice.* Allen & Unwin.

Thornton, K. (2019). Leadership in the early years: Challenges and opportunities. *New Zealand Annual Review of Education*, 24, 42–57. https://doi.org/10.26686/nzaroe.v24i0.6327

Thornton, K., Wansbrough, D., Clarkin-Phillips, J., Aitken, H., & Tamati, A. (2009). *Conceptualising leadership in early childhood education in Aotearoa New Zealand. Occasional paper.* New Zealand Teachers Council.

Wenger, E. C. (2000). Communities of practice and social learning systems. *Organization, 7*(2), 225–246. https://doi.org/10.1177/135050840072002

Wenger, E. C., & Snyder, W. M. (2000). Communities of practice: The organizational frontier. *Harvard Business Review, Jan–Feb,* 139–145.

Chapter 8

Growing associate teachers' capacity to be leaders: Recognising effective leadership during practicum

Debbie Woolston and Claire Wilson

Introduction

Practicum experiences are a key component of Initial Teacher Education (ITE) programmes, and the role of the associate teacher (AT) is one of the main identifiable factors for a successful practicum (Beck & Kosnik, 2000; Grudnoff, 2011; Woolston & Dayman, 2022). ATs have leadership capabilities and skills that are often not recognised or are overlooked simply because they feel this role is part of their professional responsibilities during practicum. Many ATs view their role of guiding tauira (student/s) as an everyday and normal part of their active practice and hold the attitude that, when they were undertaking their teaching qualification, someone, often an experienced teacher, took the time to guide them through their journey of learning to become a teacher. ATs often view this role as a way of reciprocating or paying their time forward to benefit tauira, and the wider teaching profession in general. They may not view that their specific role as an AT is centred within the vein of leadership (Wilson, 2016; Woolston, 2019). However, many effective leadership attributes are foregrounded and can be drawn out of the ATs position as they navigate this significant role as mentor, coach, and leader alongside their tauira.

The practicum experience can be a space that is perceived as a short and intense time—and a potential breeding ground for misinformation

(Clarke et al., 2014; Wilson, 2016). This is due to the many factors that are being juggled during practicum. Over a few short weeks, the AT is trying to ensure the tauira meets the academic requirements of differing tertiary providers, as well as undergoing the mammoth task of sharing and articulating the culture of their setting. Meanwhile, the tauira is operating at pace trying to find their sense of belonging; to gain an understanding of a completely new teaching team and teaching/learning paradigm; and to make relational bonds with the AT, tamariki, whānau, and other kaiako. With all this short and intense juggling taking place, this leaves plenty of room for unclear messages that can be transmitted and/or perceived between the AT and the tauira during this period. ATs mitigate these potential risks by continuing to develop their leadership competence.

There is evidence that practicum is one of the most influential times of the tauira journey into the paradigm of teaching and learning. It also holds and boasts the most weighty and critical professional growth across the spectrum of their qualification (Aspden et al., 2021). Therefore, in this practicum space, the leadership capabilities and skills of ATs can be naturally brought to the fore of their practice. The way in which this professional responsibility morphs into a leadership role is largely unrecognised by ATs themselves; hence, supporting and engaging early childhood ATs' ability and capacity to identify as leaders is beneficial to the ATs, early childhood education (ECE) settings, and the wider ECE sector (Douglass, 2018).

This chapter will highlight the effective leadership capabilities and skills that ATs utilise, implement, and grow during the teaching practicum experience. From the authors' experiences of engaging in professional discussions with many ATs, and their own respective research undertaken to complete their Master of Education studies, they have chosen to focus on five areas:

- relationships
- communication
- mentoring
- ako
- vulnerability.

These five areas are discussed below.

Relationships

Previous research has shown that, during the practicum experience, a key function of the AT is to cultivate professional and collaborative relationships between themselves, the tauira, other kaiako, tamariki, and whānau (Education Council New Zealand, 2017; Graves, 2010; Haigh et al., 2006). The AT's ability to establish and maintain these relationships is essential for the tauira and the other kaiako in the setting to experience success during their practicum experience (Turnbull, 2005). ATs often recognise the practicum experience as one where they can build trusting, caring, reciprocal relationships with tauira that promote professional growth and identity through real-life experiences. Positive practicum experiences lead to further commitment to the teaching profession by both tauira and ATs. The professional skills and attributes of such relationship building are fundamental to an AT taking on the role. However, research also indicates that having tauira in their centres allows for many other benefits (Puroila et al., 2021). The practicum experience can allow ATs to work with tauira with different personalities and from different backgrounds. It also allows ATs to develop skills around supporting emotional competence where tauira may feel under pressure due to the short time frame of the practicum experience (Puroila et al., 2021).

The ability to build relationships and demonstrate communication skills is a fundamental aspect for the AT role and also apply to leadership in all fields of employment including education. One aspect of developing leadership is the understanding and acknowledgement of leadership awareness. Leadership is deemed to be part of the role of being a kaiako in Aotearoa New Zealand (Education Council New Zealand, 2017; Education Council New Zealand, 2018a: Education Council New Zealand, 2018b). Kaiako should be aware that leadership is not just based on "positional titles" or having power over others, but rather the sense of their own leadership capability and identity. This view is simply that leadership can be carried out by kaiako regardless of their position or role. For example, leadership can be perceived as part of their everyday work and teaching responsibilities and not related to recognition as being in a leadership position. There are certain leadership styles used across all education, business, and management sectors. The leadership style can be viewed as either people-orientated or task-orientated, and overall wording may include transformational, transactional, authoritative, delegative, laissez-faire, servant, authentic, ethical, and charismatic (Rodd, 2013; Sekhar Das & Pattanayak, 2023). Regardless of the leadership style, they all rely on the forming of relationship bonds, human connection, and open forums for moving forward. Current literature supports and strengthens the growing trend and view that in ECE there is a shared or distributed form of leadership that allows kaiako to have key roles and the ability to influence change rather than it being related directly to power and authority. Often, these leadership styles require leaders to form strong relationships, trust, and connections to be successful. This perspective aligns with the expectations of the AT, as it is important they form a positive relationship with the tauira during practicum, because it can "make or break" situations and the overall practicum experience.

Communication

Communication is the other "mechanism" that supports the relationship and professional learning between the AT and student teacher (Woolston & Dayman, 2022, p. 38). Key components of effective communication include asking and answering questions, listening, advising, engaging in professional discussions, providing feedback, and allowing opportunities for reasoning and problem solving that can support the outcomes of the practicum experience (La Paro et al., 2018; McDonald & Flint, 2011; Quinones et al., 2019). Overall, the AT is seen as a professional role model who directly or indirectly leads through their own knowledge and life experiences, personal traits and attitudes, and practice (Sawalhi & Chaaban, 2022).

Overall, the influence of relationships and communication on kaiako leadership through the actions of the AT affects tauira by influencing and changing their attitudes, increasing their motivation, promoting their self-esteem, and supporting their overall wellbeing. The AT can also influence the tauira/students' judgement, ethics, reflection, and willingness to explore opportunities and experiment within their teaching practice during practicum (Chaaban & Sawalhi, 2020: Sawalhi & Chaaban, 2022).

Mentoring

Mentoring is a term that is accepted in the field of education and is commonly used in relation to tauira and beginning kaiako. It is an approach to working with tauira and beginning kaiako based on preparation and the shared understanding of requirements around the practicum experience, including roles and responsibilities of ATs, other kaiako, tauira, placement centres, and ITE providers (Grudnoff, 2011). Aspden (2015) says that in the practicum context there is still the twofold role of mentor and assessor; for example, a mentoring role with assessment responsibilities. However, Aspden's (2015) research found that ATs viewed guiding and mentoring of tauira and beginning kaiako as the main focus of the AT role (Murphy & Thornton, 2015). Mentoring can also be viewed as the means by which ATs can influence tauira growth and development and they aim to improve teaching and learning pedagogy and ideally increase their tauira learning and achievement through their practicum experience (York-Barr & Duke, 2004).

Mentoring is typically seen as a relationship between an experienced, competent individual and a less experienced individual. The experienced individual usually plays an intentional, guiding role that is also supportive, nurturing, and provides learning opportunities for the less-experienced individual (Wong & Waniganayake, 2013). In the practicum experience, the authors believe mentoring is influential in nature and therefore can be perceived as leadership in the practicum space. This is supported by Rodd (2013) as she states that mentoring is a leadership strategy to enhance competence, expand professional potential, and progress the ATs career. It also allows ATs to promote leadership capacity in other kaiako and tauira.

The mentoring role of ATs can be broken down into these sections: roles and responsibilities; skills and knowledge; and qualities and dispositions (Wong & Waniganayake, 2013). Both leadership and mentoring roles involve influencing others and, as stated above, high-trust relationships and communication are vital aspects of these roles. Leaders and mentors possess distinctive professional qualities, values, and perspectives grounded in their life and education experiences; for example, the AT's training, further study, different roles, and overall commitment of wanting "to give something back" to the ECE teaching profession. It is important that mentors have characteristics including: facilitation skills; the ability to listen; and the ability to empower others. They also need to demonstrate respect for others, trustworthiness, the ability to be both affirming and challenging, flexibility, and the ability to be reflective and show vision (Kenney et al., 2022; Quinones et al., 2019; Sawalhi & Chaaban, 2021). These qualities and attributes are woven through their practice and are a solid foundation for their own pedagogy and knowledge. These skills allow ATs to be effective in building relationships and communication, leading them to be able to gain trust, give guidance, role-model, encourage professional dialogue and reflection, and assist tauira to build their own positive relationships and practice within their practicum.

Modelling is a component of mentoring. When it is utilised by ATs, along with collective and collaborative leadership, it displays actions of taking responsibility, holding a shared vision, and promoting professional attitudes. Modelling also fosters dispositions of empowerment, self-efficacy, and motivation for tauira (Sutcliffe, 2021). Leadership and mentoring characteristics can also be identified and linked by emotional intelligence which is seen through a graceful leadership viewpoint which includes having self-awareness, motivation, vision, and empathy, and being authentic in one's professional manner (Kenney et al., 2022). The AT is well placed to support tauira to gain confidence, influence change, examine current ideas, and experience professional dialogue and reflection if the attributes discussed above are evident in their practice. The practicum experience provides opportunities for tauira to have a variety of practical experiences and expand on their theoretical knowledge. In the wider context, the AT role within practicum can support tauira to make the transition from the ITE provider environment to the workplace and also influence tauira as to who they aspire to be within their career in ECE (Sawalhi & Chaaban, 2021).

Ako

Ako is a concept from te ao Māori (the Māori world) that represents both teaching and learning, and values the knowledge contributions of both tauira and kaiako (Hemara, 2000). Ako also provides the tauira and kaiako with a non-hierarchical space for mutual learning interactivity, and for new knowledge, connections, and understandings to grow through shared learning experiences.

Ako works to bring both participants into and out of leading the knowledge transmission and acquisition processes between them (Bishop & Berryman, 2009; Edwards, 2013; Wilson, 2016). Therefore, this style of social negotiation and shared learning, within a teaching and learning setting, leads both active participants towards co-constructing and negotiating a sense of ownership. ATs who engage in ako with their tauira facilitate a sense of truth and knowing into co-operative learning and teaching situations, as they are both afforded opportunities from an equitable footing with leading, learning, and imparting wisdom (Wilson, 2016).

In a sense, ako heralds the turning or changing of mindsets for ATs—from thinking that the practicum experience offers opportunities to engage and connect with their own professional responsibilities, to recognising and growing their own leadership capacity and skills. Adopting a growth mindset can encourage a cyclic pattern of leading, reflecting, changing, and a following of ideas, practices, and skills for both the AT and the tauira. ATs who work from a space of ako nurture and connect to their own growth mindset, and draw on a combination of skills, creating a duality of challenge that establishes a joint, supportive, and reciprocated leaderful climate (Lee et al., 2022). The importance of utilising and implementing ako within active teaching practices sets the foundations for ATs to engage in acts of leadership. The dual value of working within a space of ako is that it breeds a continuous flow of learning and growing for both the AT and the tauira as both participants are afforded the opportunities to teach and contribute, and to offer new ideas and new learning perspectives, while also inspiring each other throughout the process (Tu'imana, 2022).

An example of ako is provided by Tu'imana (2022), a primary school leader in Tāmaki Makaurau/Auckland, who discusses *tauhivā ako* (a nurturing, connected space), in relation to engaging Indigenous relationships in schools. Tauhivā ako is a Tongan perspective of the "kaiako leading and learning interchange"—where, loosely translated, *tauhi* means to care for or nurture, and *vā* is a space that is created by mutual participants, places, and things. Therefore, links can be made with tauhivā ako and the AT's role as the provision of a paradigm where leadership can be fluid, but also heightened, with the new wisdom and knowledge that is continually layered upon and offered throughout the interchange of communication between participants.

Throughout the duration of the practicum, ATs who are willing to be open to both receiving and offering new ideas, whilst building on their current knowledge and wisdom, are growing increasingly leaderful in their respective roles through embracing the practices of ako.

Vulnerability

Effective leadership capabilities and skills can grow as ATs become comfortable with being vulnerable. Despite this, vulnerability can often be viewed in relation to concepts of negativity for individuals, and perceptions of being a failure and holding a weakness of character (Christodoulidi, 2023). ATs, either knowingly or unknowingly, may undergo a process of self-vulnerability as the nature of the teaching practicum challenges their capability as a teacher and leader. ATs can be vulnerable when they place their own practices, values, and beliefs on display—to be in a sense checked against teaching codes and standards alongside both tauira and visiting lecturers during practicum. Research suggests that ATs hold vital information that, when shared, enables tauira to take the initiative and grow confidence within the teaching and learning space during practicum (Wilson, 2016). Both participants who are engaged in the teaching and learning space during practicum (tauira and visiting lecturers) are from outside of the direct community of learners. This places ATs in a vulnerable position. ATs are faced with leading and mentoring the tauira so they may learn about the teaching and learning setting and develop their teaching skills with confidence, but at the same time, ATs are pushed into a space of vulnerability as they must share their own teaching praxis on what some may potentially feel as being left on "a plate for dissection" by both the tauira and visiting lecturers. Growing an openness to connect with one's own vulnerability offers many pathways for individuals to grow past an internal solitary consciousness towards a purpose for external engagement (Christodoulidi, 2023). Therefore, ATs who are comfortable with a level of vulnerability in their roles are most likely to display a strength of character, know who they are, teach with integrity, accept challenges, and are intuitive of when and where to change. Karayel (2021) frames six pillars of inclusive intelligence in relation to role-modelling diversity and inclusion within the workplace. One of these pillars focuses on self-awareness, vulnerability, and humility. ATs who role-model being or becoming vulnerable demonstrate a quality that benefits tauira across their educational pathway. Observing this enables tauira to make direct links with kaiako who display the qualities they promote (Christodoulidi, 2023). It appears that ATs who become comfortable with their own vulnerability within their roles develop capacity for effective leadership.

Becoming vulnerable also requires courage, a relinquishing of power, and the ability to be open to new suggestions and ideas. Through exploring both the challenges and opportunities in relation to changing power dynamics, ATs and tauira can begin to create spaces where inclusivity and empowerment can be nurtured and foregrounded (Brantmeier & McKenna, 2020). ATs must bring a level of bravery into their respective roles, as mentioned previously. They must step out, open their own active practices, and share their experiences for tauira to observe, judge, and sometimes replicate. But within the realms of vulnerability, ATs also have opportunities to courageously grow and nurture the skills and knowledge needed alongside tauira from a personal space to a much more communal one; as they encourage, mentor, coach, watch, listen, and engage with their tauira. Most kaiako know that teaching is a vocation. In understanding this aspect, ATs are involved in the process and preparation for the tauira to begin successfully navigating and coming to grips with both the intricacies and complexities involved in the art of the teaching profession. These acts are acts of leadership.

Conclusion

There appears to still be apprehension from ATs within the ECE sector around their recognition as leaders in this space due to the avoidance of discussions in relation to leadership. Furthermore, the misunderstanding and misconceptions about leadership in ECE often leads to the inability to recognise leadership as part of practice in everyday environments (Cooper, 2014). The authors contend it would be advantageous for ATs to draw attention to recognising and reaffirming that, through their skills and "active practice efficiencies", they are already showing leadership, and that this is something to be upheld and acknowledged.

More internal thought and reflection on ATs and what they bring to this space would enhance their practice. This would highlight their own awareness in relation to their teaching practices, but also that of how their leaderful capabilities can grow and be nurtured. This highlights the importance of continuing to grow the self-belief that they are contributing to the leadership paradigm during the teaching practicum experience. Teaching and leadership need to be viewed simultaneously and not be recognised as separate practices in the AT role. Expanding on ATs' recognition of leadership during the practicum experience would be an area that would benefit the ECE teaching profession. Future investment of resources in the areas of mentoring, growing leadership capabilities, and recognition of the time ATs spend on the role, will benefit the leadership role during practicum. Expanding on this further, opportunities to promote discussion that challenges the traditional role of leadership needs to be undertaken to promote the view of alternative leadership perspectives and leadership identities.

The utilisation and implementation of the skills and capabilities for increased growth in the leadership paradigm for ATs discussed in this chapter are just small fragments of the many effective leadership practices shown by ATs. The role of the AT is complex and intricate. ATs' ability to navigate, guide, and accomplish a successful experience throughout a finite passage of time encourages ATs into a space where they are showcasing and developing leadership capabilities and skills. The authors consider this is something to be acknowledged, respected, and celebrated.

References

Aspden, K. (2015). Dual roles: Mentoring and assessment in the early childhood practicum. In C. Murphy & K. Thornton (Eds.), *Mentoring in early childhood education: A compilation of thinking, pedagogy and practice* (pp. 105–118). NZCER Press.

Aspden, K., Broadley, M-L., Cameron, M., Turton, L. A., McClew, J., & Hopkins, R. (2021). The Tāmaki Makaurau associate teacher's network. A reflection of a decade+ of AT support. *Early Education, 67*, 75–79.

Beck, C., & Kosnik, C. (2000). Associate teachers in pre-service education: Clarifying and enhancing their role. *Journal of Education for Teaching, 26*(3), 207–224.

Bishop, R., & Berryman, M. (2009). Te kotahitanga effective teaching profile. *Set: Research Information for Teachers,* (2), 27–32. https://doi.org/10.18296/set.0461

Brantmeier, E. J., & McKenna, M. K. (2020). *Pedagogy of vulnerability.* Information Age Publishing.

Chaaban, Y., & Sawalhi, R. (2020). The role of agency in the development of a teacher leadership stance among student teachers during the practicum experience. *Research in Post- Compulsory Education, 25*(2), 171–192. https://doi.org/10.1080/13596748.2020.1742987

Christodoulidi, F. (2023). A pedagogy of vulnerability: Its relevance to diversity teaching and 'humanising' higher education. *Equity in Education & Society, 3*(2)101–113. https://doi.org/10.1177/27526461231185834

Clarke, A., Triggs, V., & Nielsen, W. (2014). Cooperating teacher participation in teacher education. A review of the literature. *Review of Educational Research, 88*(2), 113–202.

Cooper, M. (2014). 'Everyday teacher leadership': A reconceptualization for early childhood education. *Journal of Educational Leadership, Policy and Practice, 29*(2), 84–96.

Douglass, A. (2018). Redefining leadership: Lessons from an early education leadership development initiative. *Early Childhood Education Journal, 46*, 387–396. https://doi.org/10.1007/s10643-017-0871-9

Education Council New Zealand. (2017). *Our code our standards: Code of professional responsibility and standards for the teaching profession.* https://teachingcouncil.nz/professional-practice/our-code-our-standards/

Education Council New Zealand (2018a). *The leadership strategy for the teaching profession of Aotearoa New Zealand: Enabling every teacher to develop their leadership capability| Te rautaki kaihautū mō te umanga whakaakoranga o Aotearoa: Kia āhei ia kaiako ki te whakawhanake i ōna pūkenga kaihautū*. Author. https://teachingcouncil.nz/assets/Files/Leadership-Strategy/Leadership_Strategy.pdf

Education Council New Zealand (2018b). *Education Leadership Capability Framework*. Author. https://teachingcouncil.nz/assets/Files/Leadership-Strategy/Leadership_Capability_Framework.pdf

Edwards, S. (2013). Ako wānanga: The art of science and spiritual endeavour of teaching and learning in a wānanga: A localised approach. *International Journal of Pedagogical Innovations, 1*(2), 69–73.

Graves, S. (2010). Mentoring pre-service teachers: A case study. *Australian Journal of Early Childhood, 35*(4), 14–20.

Grudnoff, L. (2011). Rethinking the practicum: Limitations and possibilities. *Asia–Pacific Journal of Teacher Education, 39*(3), 223–234.

Haigh, M., Pinder, H., & McDonald, L. (2006, September). *Practicum's contribution to students' learning to teach*. Paper presented at the British Educational Research Association Annual Conference, University of Warwick, United Kingdom.

Hemara, W. (2000). *Māori pedagogies. A view from the literature*. NZCER Press.

Karayel, F. (2021). *Inclusive intelligence: How to be a role model for diversity and inclusion in the workplace*. Panoma Press.

Kenney, C., Dorfman, A., & Thwaite, S. (2022). Learning to lead: Lessons taken from the wisest people we know. *Journal of Curriculum, Teaching, Learning, and Leadership Education, 7*(1), 12–25.

La Paro, K. M., Van Schagen, A., King, E., & Lippard, C. (2018). A systems perspective on practicum experiences in early childhood teacher education: Focus on interprofessional relationships. *Early Childhood Education Journal, 46*, 365–375. https://doi.org/10.1007/s10643-017-0872-8

Lee, Y., Douglass, A., Zeng, S., Wiehe-Lopez, A., & Reyes, A. (2022). Preparing early educators as frontline leaders and change agents with a leadership development initiative. *International Journal of Child Care and Education Policy, 16*(2), 1–18. https://doi.org/10.1186/s40723-022-00095-z

McDonald, L., & Flint, A. (2011). Effective educative mentoring skills: A collaborative effort. *New Zealand Journal of Teachers Work, 8*(1), 33–46.

Murphy, C., & Thornton, K. (Eds). (2015). *Mentoring in early childhood education: A compilation of thinking, pedagogy and practice*. NZCER Press.

Puroila, A-M., Kupila, P., & Pekkarinen, A. (2021). Multiple facets of supervision: Cooperative teachers' views of supervision in early childhood teacher education practicums. *Teaching and Teacher Education, 105*(103413), 1–12. https://doi.org/10.1016/j.tate.2021.103413

Quinones, G., Rivalland, C., & Monk, H. (2019). Mentoring positioning: Perspectives of early childhood mentors. *Asia–Pacific Journal of Teacher Education, 48*(4), 338–354. https://doi.org/10.1080/1359866X.2019.1644610

Rodd, J. (2013). *Leadership in early childhood: The pathway to professionalism* (4th ed.). Allen & Unwin.

Sawalhi, R., & Chaaban, Y. (2021). Mentor teachers' and student teachers' perspectives toward teacher leadership. *Mentoring & Tutoring: Partnership in Learning, 29*(1), 70–88. https://doi.org/10.1080/13611267.2021.1899586

Sawalhi R., & Chaaban, Y. (2022). Student teachers' perspectives towards teacher leadership. *International Journal of Leadership in Education, 25*(4), 586–602.

Sekhar Das, S., & Pattanayak, S. (2023). Understanding the effect of leadership styles on employee well-being through leader-member exchange. *Current Psychology, 42*, 21310–21325. https://doi.org/10.1007/s12144-022-03243-3

Sutcliffe, T. (2021). Enacting teacher leadership. *Swings and Roundabouts,* 20–21.

Tu'imana, 'E. (2022). Tauhivā ako: Engaging indigenous relationality in school leadership. *Ethnographic Edge, 5*(2), 1–19.

Turnbull, M. (2005). Student teacher professional agency in the practicum. *Asia–Pacific Journal of Teacher Education, 33*(2), 195–208.

Wilson, C. M. (2016). *Creating effective invited spaces: Putting the lens on early childhood teacher education practica.* [Master's thesis, Massey University].

Wong, D., & Waniganayake, M. (2013). Mentoring as a leadership development strategy in early childhood education. In E. Hujala, M Waniganayake, & J. Rodd (Eds.), *Researching leadership in early childhood education* (pp. 163–180). Tampere University Press.

Woolston, D. (2019). Understanding the motivation of associate teachers in early childhood education. *Early Childhood Folio, 23*(2), 24–28. https://doi.org/10.18296/ecf.0067

Woolston, D., & Dayman, T. (2022). Practicum: A space for leadership and mentoring. *New Zealand Journal of Teachers' Work, 19*(1), 29–45. https://doi.org/10.24135/teacherswork.v19i1.335

York-Barr, J., & Duke, K. (2004). What do we know about teacher leadership? Findings from two decades of scholarship. *Review of Educational Research, 74*(3), 255–316.

PART 3

LEADERSHIP WITHIN THE PRIMARY SCHOOL SECTOR

Chapter 9

Leading primary schools in Aotearoa New Zealand: The role and challenges of school leaders

J Clark McPhillips and Tracey Carlyon

Introduction

The term "school leadership", while traditionally focused on the role of the school principal, has been broadened to include others who hold leadership roles in schools (Youngs, 2020). Certainly, the role and expectations of school leaders have become much wider and multifaceted (Wylie, 2020). Twenty years ago, Upsall (2004) cautioned school leaders would need to be "superhuman" to cope with the demands of the role and it does seem that little has changed since. School leaders still have overall responsibility for finances, property, health and safety, strategic direction, reporting, and human resources. They are also responsible for the day-to-day functions of a school and for managing multiple demands from various stakeholders, communities, organisations, and governing bodies. Further to these demands, school leaders in Aotearoa New Zealand are also required to be the leaders of learning in their schools.

Research from Aotearoa New Zealand has focused on developing best practice for school leaders. This has included the *School Leadership and Student Outcomes: Identifying What Works and Why Best Evidence Synthesis Iteration* (BES) (Robinson et al., 2009) and *Tū Rangatira— Māori Medium Educational Leadership* (Ministry of Education, 2010). While well over 10 years old, both remain relevant and continue to inform school leaders in the present day. More recent publications include *Our Schooling Futures: Stronger Together* (Tomorrow's Schools

Independent Taskforce, 2018). Appointed by the Minister of Education at the time, the Taskforce conducted a review of the compulsory school system to establish whether a case for change should be made. In the same year, during consultation on the draft Leadership Strategy for the Teaching Profession, the Education Council of Aotearoa New Zealand (now the Teaching Council of Aotearoa New Zealand) commissioned the New Zealand Council for Educational Research (NZCER) to develop the *Educational Leadership Capability Framework* (Education Council New Zealand, 2018). The intention was to support the Leadership Strategy to advance educational leadership in Aotearoa New Zealand. Additionally, the implementation of the first-time principal package, postgraduate leadership programmes, and principal appraisal process, and the development of Kāhui Ako | Communities of Learning have also provided useful and continued guidance for school leaders.

Given the influence of school leadership on student learning (Robinson & Gray, 2019), it is important to understand the role of school leaders and how they effectively navigate all aspects of this. Within the unique context of Aotearoa New Zealand, schools and school leaders have an obligation to provide equal opportunity to raise the achievement for underperforming groups, such as Māori, Pacific people, and students with additional learning needs. To support school leaders in their role, advice is provided by the Ministry of Education and external evaluation by the Education Review Office for all English- and Māori-medium schools in Aotearoa New Zealand. Alongside this, the *National Education Learning Priorities* (*NELP*) places learners at the centre along with barrier-free access, quality teaching and leadership, future of learning and work, and world-class inclusive public education (Ministry of Education, 2020). To ensure school leaders meet these priorities, it is essential that ongoing guidance is provided and research relevant to the current leadership context is undertaken.

Despite the research and guidance provided for school leaders, concern regarding the expectations of school leaders, their wellbeing, and the lack of ongoing systemic support has increased in Aotearoa New Zealand (Wylie, 2020). Similarly, research from Australia has highlighted "unsustainable adverse health outcomes" for school leaders due to their high workload, which leaves them a lack of time to focus on teaching and learning (Branson et al., 2024, p. 219). To contribute to the body of research, the small-scale study on which this chapter is informed was undertaken in 2023 to gain a greater understanding of the role and challenges of school leaders. The chapter first presents a brief outline of the study. Then findings from the study are discussed, together with relevant literature, within two discussion sections; first, how school leaders see their role; and second, the challenges school leaders currently face. The subheadings in each of these sections are representative of the themes derived from the study.

The study

The study explored the experiences of nine school leaders from a range of different primary school contexts in Aotearoa New Zealand. The qualitative research involved the school leaders participating in one semistructured interview each. The participants all held primary school principal positions at the time of the study. In composition, they were broadly reflective of the 2019 primary and secondary school principal workforce in Aotearoa New Zealand (Jagger, 2020). Purposive sampling was used to select participants who were diverse in gender, age, ethnicity, time served as a principal, school roll size, and the geographical location of school. The semistructured interviews were conducted face to face and were audio recorded for later transcription and analysis. To protect the anonymity of the participants, each was allocated an identification number and referred to with the preface Pn. The following questions provided prompts for the participants to draw on their own leadership experiences and guided the study:

1. What are the key responsibilities and functions of a leader?
2. What kind of leadership process and structures do schools have in place that enable school leaders to fulfil their role effectively?
3. What are the challenges school leaders face in their role?

How school leaders see their role

The role of school leaders in Aotearoa New Zealand is multidimensional and complex, and often requires working long hours to manage workload (Tomorrow's Schools Independent Taskforce, 2018). The study provided evidence to support this and highlighted three common themes pertaining to how the participants saw their roles as primary school leaders. These themes, which are discussed next, include: the tension between CEO and leader of learning roles; ensuring wellbeing and establishing relational trust; and developing leadership capability.

Tension between CEO and leader of learning roles

The clear difference between other OECD countries and Aotearoa New Zealand is its system of self-managing schools, which requires school leaders to work as CEOs of their boards of trustees in addition to leading the learning (Ministry of Education, 2008). For example, the Educational Leadership Model (ELM) requires school leaders to have knowledge and skills of systems, partnerships and networks, culture and pedagogy in order to lead 21st century schools (Ministry of Education, 2008). The model, which is underpinned by research evidence and was developed by the Ministry of Education after extensive consultation, is still current today. Yet, despite the clear indications of school leaders' work in the model, the study highlighted a clear tension that existed between the CEO and leader of learning roles. This tension was created as the participants were constantly seeking ways to balance the two competing roles, and while it could be considered that leading the learning is part of the CEO role, they clearly did not share this view. It was evident that a significant amount of their time and energy was spent in the CEO role, as they managed aspects from strategic planning to finances and property. For instance, P2 explained, "As a school leader, you easily get lost in all the paperwork and not actually lead the school". An example of this was provided by P9, who stated that, "You've got to know everything about safety. Safety is huge. The evacuations, you've got to know about police vetting, you've got to know about EOTC". Although these aspects are part of the school leader's role, it was pointed out by P4 that most are not trained in finance, law, or human resources. This viewpoint was supported by P3, who said, "The job description isn't accurate to what you actually do". The role of the school leader was further summarised by P2 as, "meeting the expectations in terms of the National Education Learning Priorities, our strategic plan, and then delivering so that it's at the coalface with our students". These comments support Jones (2022), who contends school leaders are required to balance a range of different aspects of their role within the everyday management of their schools.

Despite the CEO role consuming much of their time, the participants all considered their priority was to be leaders of learning. Their responses showed all were fully aware of the importance of getting the right balance in their role to ensure there were no detrimental outcomes for the students, school community, or themselves. Additionally, they reiterated that, when the focus shifted from students and learning, then school leaders needed to question their role. P4 gave this example: "Every day I finish each day with a mantra, what have I done for children today? What have I done for our learners today?". Further to this, both P3 and P6 pointed out that being a leader of learning required being in touch with both staff and students on a daily basis. P4 explained they had to be nimble to balance both roles and be physically present in the school. It became apparent that, while there is a very real tension between aspects of their roles, school leaders are clearly committed to being leaders of learning. This aligns with the claim that successful school leaders are adaptable and can "respond to context and not be subservient to it" (Constantinides, 2023, p. 7).

Ensuring wellbeing and establishing relational trust

An essential aspect of the school leader's role is supporting the wellbeing of students and staff (Day et al., 2020) in addition to establishing relational trust (Branson et al., 2024; Le Fevre, 2010). In support of this, ensuring the wellbeing of both students and staff was expressed by all participants as being paramount to the success of learners within their schools. P2 highlighted this, saying, "Hauora, wellbeing of our students, wellbeing with our staff … if you've got those things sorted then you can get on with the teaching". Moreover, since COVID-19, the level of support needed for students and staff wellbeing seemed to have increased. This is not surprising, given the increased sense of responsibility teachers have for their students' wellbeing since COVID-19 (Dharan et al., 2022). Furthermore, as P5 reflected, "Five years ago [staff] tended to take a bit more responsibility for [their] own wellbeing", while they noticed now there is an expectation that school leaders will take care of staff wellbeing. It is important to acknowledge the ongoing support for students' and staff wellbeing that has been required from school leaders since COVID-19.

Notably, the participants were aware of the demands teachers face, including delivering the curriculum and dealing with societal issues that impact students. In addition, they were cognisant of the impact these demands had on the wellbeing of their staff and felt a responsibility to minimise pressure, particularly on teachers, to support their wellbeing. This was articulated by P4, who stated:

> We don't burden them [teachers] with a lot of that … we can take that stuff off them, do the heavy lifting as it were, to let them bring the energy and vibe and excitement and drive and be the very best that they can be in the classroom.

However, to support staff and student wellbeing it is essential school leaders develop relational trust by demonstrating integrity, honesty, and openness (Anaru, 2018; Branson et al., 2024). The participants' responses indicated that, in order to focus on wellbeing, the school leader must show they value relational trust by developing and modelling trusting relationships and behaviours expected within the school (Le Fevre, 2010). P7 felt strongly about this when interviewed and suggested, "(It's) about building trust, and that takes time … and acting with integrity. Without this type of trust within the school environment the optimal environment for learning won't happen". The challenge of maintaining relational trust was also raised by the participants who reiterated the importance of school leaders making a deliberate effort to be visible to students and staff.

As was the case in this study, previous studies have highlighted that effective school leaders understand the importance of their own wellbeing (Constantinides, 2023; Notman & Henry, 2011). In particular, those participants who had held school leadership roles for more than 20 years understood the importance of paying attention to their own wellbeing to support them to continue in their current positions. Reference was made to the importance of physical and mental health and taking time out of school for activities such as sabbaticals, holidays, travel, family, sport, and hobbies. When this does not occur, and school leaders fail to prioritise their own wellbeing over competing school demands, this can impact on their families and personal lives (Notman & Henry, 2011). P7 pointed out that "principals themselves, they need to make sure that they do keep themselves physically fit … as a way of managing stress levels". Research has highlighted that, when school leaders pay specific attention to their own physical and mental wellbeing, this contributes to their sustained success (Constantinides, 2023).

Developing leadership capability

In line with Fullan's (2003) claim that developing leadership capability in others is a moral imperative of school leadership, the study confirmed the important role school leaders play. School leaders identify potential in others, model effective leadership practice, and establish an environment inclusive of relational trust for leadership capability to grow within schools (Fisher & Carlyon, 2014). This was evident in the study, in which all participants acknowledged the importance of developing leadership capability among their staff. As P8 expressed, "I'm building leadership capacity in my place, so that I don't have to be the fount of all knowledge and expertise, because I'm not". These findings aligned to other research, such as that conducted by Fisher and Carlyon (2014), who found that recognising and developing leadership capability in others can occur in a number of different ways and is an important part of the school leader's role. One example was provided by P5, who stated:

> It's looking at identifying leaders and growing people. We've just got a new teacher that's come into the school, and I can see some leadership in her. So, I've had a quick chat to her about maybe leading a bit more

of the Year 7 and 8s next year, so we have a bit more structure in the year, and she's really keen.

Another example of developing leadership capability was provided by P6, who attributed their own career development into school leadership by surrounding themselves with leaders who modelled effective leadership practice and mentored them until they were ready: "They constantly took me under their wing until I got my principalship". In contrast, P2 noted it had become more common for teachers to step into school leadership after a short period of teaching. As a result, they were often unprepared for their new role, which P2 claimed reiterated the importance of developing leadership capability in others.

The importance of continuing to develop leadership capability within others in their schools was a high priority for the participants. P8 pointed out it was important that there were others taking leadership roles. This was taken further by P7 who considered it integral to their "moral purpose" to develop leadership capability in others. Additionally, the participants all clearly enjoyed their role and considered it to be their responsibility to provide an environment where leadership capability could be developed and nurtured. This was achieved by being collaborative in their practice and sharing opportunities for leadership amongst staff. They each explained that, while their leadership teams often comprised a traditional structure (deputy and assistant principals and/or team leaders), this structure often served the sole purpose of allowing for deputising in the school leader's absence. Taking a collaborative approach to sharing leadership provides staff with opportunities to develop leadership capability, regardless of whether they hold formally designated leadership roles (Notman, 2020). Examples of this were included in participants' comments: "even though there is that [formal] structure that we have a lot of others within the school who hold leadership positions" (P4); and, "We have a very flat structure, so there's no hierarchy here" (P5). Likewise, P9 commented: "Leadership is all of us … it isn't one person at the top". These findings provide evidence that collaborative leadership practices are often part of a broader aim of school leaders to develop leadership capability in others (Constantinides, 2023).

The challenges school leaders currently face

The study highlighted several common challenges the participants faced in their roles as primary school leaders. These included: the relentless pace and cost of compliance; inequities in resourcing, funding, and salaries; societal shifts and changing expectations; and meeting community needs.

The relentless pace and cost of compliance

In Aotearoa New Zealand, the Ministry of Education provides schools with legislative regulations to ensure they operate safely and efficiently. It is the role of the school leader to ensure the school is fully compliant with these regulations. While the participants understood the need for these regulations, the relentless pace and cost of compliance was repeatedly brought to light as being an ongoing challenge. This challenge was exacerbated by a lack of clarity and rationale, unrealistic expectations, and the time involved for school leaders to meet compliance.

An example of a Ministry of Education health and safety compliance issue was provided by P1, who explained their rural school was required to provide a regular water testing sample. The company contracted to undertake the water testing frequently submitted late samples; however, the Ministry of Education showed no flexibility or understanding towards the school regarding this. Other participants provided similar examples, including P4 who pointed out the "phenomenal amount of paperwork" required to meet health and safety requirements for school camps, which jeopardised such activities from occurring. The comment by P9 was reflective of all the participants in the study, who explained: "Property is a huge barrier. And we've got a property manager … That's a huge part of our board meeting is property, every month, more than talking about learning or anything. It's property". Undoubtedly, time spent by school leaders on compliance has the unintended consequences of distancing them from their role as leaders of learning (Barker, 2023; Tomorrow's Schools Independent Taskforce, 2018).

Complying with reporting requirements was raised by the participants as being challenging and complex. They attributed much of this challenge to the unrealistic time frames they were frequently given to gain adequate consultation and complete reporting. In addition, the constant communication from the Ministry of Education relating to compliance was also highlighted by the participants, such as in the following comment:

> The emails are just a nightmare. It's nonstop. And I try to answer all my emails. I can't. I try to, but I inevitably miss out on something, and I feel bad, but there's just so many emails coming in, that's relentless. (P9)

Often the Ministry of Education requirements involve significant changes for schools. As P6 pointed out, "you feel like you are always behind the 8-ball ... something comes out and you've got to implement it ... change is coming faster than it did ... there's just so much on your plate now". Adding to this, P1 talked at length about the "relentless expectations and the Ministry of Education that really should be the body to support. But it seems to be working against us". Insufficient support for schools from the Ministry of Education puts extra pressure on school leaders in what is already a demanding role (Tomorrow's Schools Independent Taskforce, 2018; Wylie, 2020).

Inequities in resourcing, funding, and salaries

Despite recommendations by Tomorrow's Schools Independent Taskforce (2018) to implement an equity index system to deliver resources and a review of management and staffing entitlements to ensure they are fit for purpose, it would seem not much action has been taken. The study showed there remain a number of inequities in resourcing, funding, and salaries that have a direct impact on schools and school leaders. An example was provided by P7, who pointed out that, while some schools have the capacity to draw on international students for additional resourcing, for others this is not an option. P9 explained that valuable resources, such as support staff, are sometimes difficult to fund and their school "can only really afford four teacher aides. We probably need six". In addition, P7 explained:

> They [the ministry] put all this responsibility onto schools to cater for a wide range of neuro-diverse learners and tell us we have to do it … some of these kids need specialists to be working with them in school, and we need to have access to employing specialists to work with dyslexic kids, other neuro-diverse kids, kids with mental health issues.

Aligned with inequities previously identified in the secondary school sector, the participants commented on inadequate funding for primary schools (Macann, 2020). The following statement by P5 was reflective of others: "It has become a lot harder to access money, especially around children with special needs, or they're very limited on the ORS [Ongoing Resourcing Scheme] funding". Further to this, P9 pointed out there was a huge amount of red tape required to access funding from the Ministry of Education for specific projects, and P7 stated "there's no answer … nobody knows within the ministry". Another inequity pertaining to school leaders' remuneration was raised in the interviews, with P7 pointing out: "The ministry's model is unfit for what they want us to do" and P5 explaining that "simple things like a principal in a smaller school can get paid significantly less than a DP in a large school". Ongoing inequities in resourcing, funding, and salaries within the school system across Aotearoa New Zealand (Thrupp, 2007, 2023) create challenges for school leaders who already have a demanding role.

Societal shifts and changing expectations

Societal shifts and changing expectations also pose challenges to a school's culture and leadership (Stoll, 2000; Thrupp, 2023). Reflective of this, a number of issues were repeatedly raised by the participants as posing ongoing challenges for school leaders. These societal shifts included the influence of social media and the digital world, in addition to dealing with working families, poverty, crime, trauma, tragedy, addictions, and the impact of the COVID-19 pandemic.

The study's findings showed that the increase in students' and parents' engagement with social media and digital technology can pose challenges for school leaders. P5 drew attention to school leaders having responsibility to ensure there is a good balance between digital and traditional learning methods, and P1 discussed the challenges associated with social media use by students and parents. A further challenge raised was the impact of trauma, tragedy, and addictions on students and how this flowed onto school and school leaders. P5 explained, "Every weekend I'm dealing with family harm, notifications from the police, it's all those things". This was reiterated by P9: "It's not like we have kids that just sort of are easy to teach. They're way behind. They've had trauma, they've got poor social skills".

While less attention was given to COVID-19 in the interviews than the researchers had anticipated, it was evident that the school leader's role grew and changed during this time. As P7 explained, "COVID-19 really made it a community leadership role". The ongoing impacts of COVID-19 were raised, and the anxiety levels of both students and parents have increased. P6 commented on the impacts of COVID-19:

> We've got a whole new generation of kids coming through. We've got a whole new generation of parents coming through. There's still anxiety in the community. There are still kids that don't come to school every day. COVID families still suffering from issues, people with more anxiety, kids that seem to be more anxious.

The following response by P4 was indicative of the views of other participants: "The complexity of [children's] needs coming into schools these days is much greater than it was".

The study's findings aligned with Ranjan's (2024) research which found that expectations from parents and caregivers of school leaders have changed and at times become unrealistic. There was a common perception among the participants that school leaders are expected to adhere to everyone's requests. P1 described these expectations as "relentless … they just blame the schools for everything". Further to this, P7 attributed much of this to "parents not building resilience in their own kids, and maybe they're lacking resilience themselves". It is clear, as Notman and Henry (2009) pointed out over a decade ago, that societal shifts and pressures have changed and this has brought an expectation that school leaders will deal with issues immediately and successfully, while at the same time continuing to address the needs of all learners.

Meeting community needs

To meet their communities' needs, it is important for school leaders to build relationships, regularly consult with local community groups (Constantinides, 2023), and establish a shared vision for their schools (Day et al., 2020). The study highlighted that, to achieve this, school leaders are required to establish support and positive school community connections, while at the same time create a school vision. For Māori communities, this requires leaders to listen respectfully and respond accordingly (Berryman et al., 2015). Examples of this occurring were provided by P3, P5, and P6, each of whom had placed particular focus on breaking down barriers by encouraging their Māori communities and Pacific communities to increase engagement with the schools. P7 noted the importance of "listening to the people in the community about their vision for what their kids would need in the future, and what part of their community-togetherness they'd like to retain and how we do that on the site".

Because of the diverse range of cultural and ethnic groups included in each school community, meeting everyone's needs and expectations can be challenging for school leaders (Starr, 2022). This was reinforced in the findings, with P5 explaining that meeting these expectations "creates a lot of challenges and barriers for you, trying to get that right". Adding to this, they suggested that meeting community needs often required school leaders to play the role of a peacemaker. In addition, the importance of school leaders being visible and accessible to all community groups and creating a vision with all stakeholders for the school were all raised in the interviews. P8 articulated this well:

> I have worked really hard to create the vision for our school, which involves the community and the teachers and everyone … Our school vision revolves around what we do now for our tamariki that makes them positive contributors to a community.

In support of this, research has identified effective school leaders are those who purposefully work with their communities to establish and communicate a school vision (Day et al., 2020; Notman & Henry, 2011).

Conclusion

This chapter has reported on findings from research, involving nine primary school leaders in Aotearoa New Zealand, to gain a greater understanding of the role of school leaders. The study focused on understanding the key responsibilities and functions of a leader; leadership process and structures schools have in place that enable school leaders to fulfil their role; and the challenges school leaders face. Although there were differences in the participants' gender, age, ethnicity, term served as principal, roll size, and the school's geographical area, the study highlighted similarities in how they saw their role as school leaders and how they managed the many challenges.

Although this was a small-scale study, it became evident that the multidimensional nature of the role and the challenges faced by primary school leaders have continued to increase in both complexity and volume. In particular, the burgeoning nature of the role has resulted in, what could be argued, unrealistic expectations that school leaders must navigate as CEOs and leaders of learning. Added to this, the external advice and evaluation intended to support school leaders often leads to more pressure. Nonetheless, employing a collaborative style of leadership appears to enable school leaders to manage the challenges and balance many aspects of their role to ensure the learner stays at the centre of all decision making.

Moving forward, the question remains: in spite of everything learnt about primary school leadership in Aotearoa New Zealand over the past 35 years and more, why does the role still demand "superhuman" (Upsall, 2004) abilities? While it is evident that school leaders have a clear understanding of what is important in their role, and are committed to this, the challenges they face to be effective cannot be ignored. As such, it is critical to hear their voices, acknowledge their concerns, and take appropriate action. Much greater attention is required to ensure that support for school leaders to meet their priorities is adequate, targeted, and timely. In addition, it is essential that initiatives such as Kāhui Ako continue, as they offer school leaders opportunities to develop a collaborative and collegial voice.

References

Anaru, L. (2018). *Building relational trust.* Ministry of Education. https://www.educationalleaders.govt.nz/Leadership-development/Professional-information/Leadership-capability-framework/High-trust-relationships/Building-relational-trust

Barker, M. (2023). When tomorrow comes: Contextualising the independent review of Tomorrow's Schools. *Policy Quarterly, 19*(3), 11–18. https://doi.org/10.26686/pq.v19i3.8307

Berryman, M., Ford, T., & Egan, M. (2015). Developing collaborative connections between schools and Māori communities. *Set: Research Information for Teachers,* (3), 18–25. https://doi.org/10.18296/set.0023

Branson, C. M., Marra, M., & Kidson, K. (2024). Responding to the current capricious state of Australian educational leadership: We should have seen it coming! *Education Sciences, 4*, 410. https://doi.org/10.3390/educsci14040410

Constantinides, M. (2023). Successful school leadership in New Zealand: A scoping review. *Education Sciences, 13*(12), 1189. https://doi.org/10.3390/educsci13121189)

Day, C., Gorgen, K., & Sammons, P. (2020). *Successful school leadership.* Education Development Trust. https://www.edt.org/research-and-insights/successful-school-leadership-2020-publication/

Dharan, V., Pond, R., & Mincher, N. (2022). *Teacher and student well-being in the Covid-19 pandemic.* Massey University. https://mro.massey.ac.nz/server/api/core/bitstreams/f40cd6e6-6b73-4740-b962-d17b7ef992e4/content

Education Council New Zealand . (2018). *Educational leadership capability framework.* Teaching Council. https://teachingcouncil.nz/assets/Files/Leadership-Strategy/Leadership_Capability_Framework.pdf

Fisher, A., & Carlyon, T. (2014). School leaders growing leadership from within: A framework for the development of school leaders. *Waikato Journal of Education, 19*(2), 93–102. https://doi.org/10.15663/wje.v20i2.179

Fullan, M. (2003). *The moral imperative of school leadership.* SAGE Publications.

Jagger, D. (2020). *School principals in New Zealand.* Ministry of Education. https://www.educationcounts.govt.nz/publications/schooling2/workforce

Jones, L. (2022). Why many school principals are CEOs, in principle. *School principal or CEO?* Fisher Leadership. https://fisherleadership.com/school-principal-or-ceo/

Le Fevre, D. (2010). Changing tack: Talking about change knowledge for professional learning. In H. Timperley & J. Parr (Eds.), *Weaving evidence, inquiry and standards to build better schools* (pp. 71–92). NZCER Press.

Macann, G. (2020). Leadership in our secondary schools: Good people, inadequate systems. *Journal of Educational Leadership, Policy and Practice*, *35*(Special Issue), 14–24. https://doi.org/10.21307/jelpp-2020-004

Ministry of Education. (2008). *Kiwi leadership for principals*. https://www.educationalleaders.govt.nz/Leadership-development/Key-leadership-documents/Kiwi-leadership-for-principals

Ministry of Education. (2010). *Tū rangatira Māori medium educational leadership*. https://www.educationalleaders.govt.nz/Leadership-development/Key-leadership-documents/Tu-rangatira-English

Ministry of Education. (2020). *The statement of national education and learning priorities (NELP)*. https://assets.education.govt.nz/public/Documents/NELP-TES-documents/FULL-NELP-2020.pdf

Notman, R. (2020). An evolution in distributed educational leadership: From sole leader to co-principalship. *Journal of Educational Leadership, Policy and Practice*, *35*(Special Issue), 27–40. https://doi.org/10.21307/jelpp-2020-005

Notman, R., & Henry, D. A. (2009). The human face of principalship: A synthesis of case study findings. *Journal of Educational Leadership, Policy and Practice*, *24*(1), 37–52. https://search.informit.org/doi/pdf/10.3316/informit.872314902981261

Notman, R., & Henry, D. A. (2011). Building and sustaining successful school leadership in New Zealand. *Leadership and Policy in Schools*, *10*, 375–394. https://doi.org/10.1080/15700763.2011.610555

Ranjan, R. (2024, January 4). *How can you manage unrealistic expectations from parents?* Linkedin. https://www.linkedin.com/pulse/how-can-you-manage-unrealistic-expectations-from-parents-ranjan-aoakf

Robinson, V., & Gray, E. (2019). What difference does school leadership make to student outcomes? *Journal of the Royal Society of New Zealand*, *49*(2), 171–187. https://doi.org/10.1080/03036758.2019.1582075

Robinson, V., Hohepa, M., & Lloyd, C. (2009). *School leadership and student outcomes: Identifying what works and why: Best Evidence Synthesis iteration (BES)*. Ministry of Education. https://www.educationcounts.govt.nz/publications/series/2515/60170

Starr, J. P. (2022). Expectations and exceptions on leadership. *Kappan*, *104*(4), 60–61. https://doi.org/10.1177/00317217221142988

Stoll, L. (2000). School culture. *Set: Research Information for Teachers*, (3), 9–14. https://doi.org/10.18296/set.0805

Thrupp, M. (2007). Education's "inconvenient truth": Persistent middle class advantage. [An inaugural professorial lecture]. *Waikato Journal of Education*, *13*, 253–271. https://researchcommons.waikato.ac.nz/server/api/core/bitstreams/df4031b7-74dc-4409-9494-971c01a990e9/content

Thrupp, M. (2023). Education's "inconvenient truth": Part two—The middle classes have too many friends in education. *New Zealand Journal of Teachers' Work*, *20*(1), 117–125. https://doi.org/10.24135/teacherswork.v20i1.441

Tomorrow's Schools Independent Taskforce. (2018). *Our schooling futures: Stronger together*. Ministry of Education. https://conversation.education.govt.nz/assets/TSR/Tomorrows-Schools-Review-Report-13Dec2018.PDF

Upsall, D. (2004). Shared principalship of schools. *New Zealand Annual Review of Education, 13*, 143–168. https://doi.org/10.26686/nzaroe.v0i13.1452

Wylie, C. (2020). What does it mean to be a principal? A policy researcher's perspective on the last 30 years in Aotearoa New Zealand. *Journal of Educational Leadership, Policy and Practice, 35*(Special Issue), 41–58. https://doi.org/10.21307/jelpp-2020-007

Youngs, H. (2020). Thirty years of leadership in New Zealand education: From the shadows of management to sine qua non. *Journal of Educational Leadership, Policy and Practice, 35*(Special Issue), 59–77. https://doi.org/10.21307/jelpp-2020-008

Chapter 10

Successful teacher change and transition: The role of primary school leaders

Tracey Carlyon

Introduction

Leading change is considered one of the most important aspects of a school leader's role (Fullan, 2020). While change is constant in schools, it cannot be assumed that it always has a positive impact on teachers or teaching. Negative impacts of change have been well documented in the literature. A key factor for successful change, however, has been identified by other studies to be effective leadership (Fullan, 2020). Successful change encompasses a transition process, which includes a psychological shift for those involved (Bridges, 2009; Morrison & Ferrier-Kerr, 2015). This transition process involves internalising and coming to terms with any new situations that change brings about. It is therefore incumbent upon school leaders to ensure that any change for teachers is understood and carefully managed (Carlyon & Branson, 2018).

This chapter draws on the author's doctoral study, which explored how New Zealand primary school leaders can successfully facilitate change and transition for teachers moving from one class level to another and support them to understand it as an opportunity for professional learning. The study found that, although changing class levels may seem common practice in primary schools in Aotearoa New Zealand, the critical role that school leaders play in this process is often underestimated and misunderstood.

The transition between class levels, whether initiated by teachers or as part of assigning teachers to class levels, presents a unique set of challenges for school leaders. Despite its frequency, the knowledge and skills required from school leaders to facilitate this change and transition successfully are often overlooked. This chapter delves into the complexities of change and transition and emphasises the significance of effective leadership in managing the process well.

The study

The doctoral study *Exploring Teacher Transition in New Zealand Primary Schools: The Impact of Changing Class Levels on Teacher Professional Learning* (Carlyon, 2016a) aimed to build knowledge about teachers' transition between class levels in primary schools and to examine the implications of this change for teachers' professional learning. Notwithstanding the opportunities for rich professional learning afforded to teachers, or the challenges associated with changing class levels, the study revealed the role of school leaders as being integral for teachers to successfully negotiate change and transition.

The mixed-methods research involved gathering both qualitative and quantitative data that would best answer the research questions. An online survey was completed by a random sample of 536 teachers from across Aotearoa New Zealand, of whom 485 had taught more than one class level and 51 had taught only one class level. Following this, a small purposive sample of teachers from the Waikato region, all of whom had changed class levels multiple times, participated in semi-structured interviews.

Prior to the doctoral study, personal experience of changing class levels in primary schools was the impetus for the author's Master's study. This was followed by a range of research projects involving school principals and teachers which informed the doctoral study. Primarily focusing on how teachers negotiate transition, the doctoral study highlighted how the change from teaching one class level to another could be viewed as a valuable opportunity for rich professional learning for teachers (Carlyon & Fallon, 2017).

Changing class levels: An opportunity for rich professional learning

Teachers, at different times during their careers, require diverse opportunities to access and make sense of new knowledge and information (Livingston, 2012) and to foster a fresh outlook on teaching (Carlyon & Fisher, 2013). Although sometimes overlooked as an opportunity for professional learning, changing class levels, and the associated transition, has been shown to have a positive impact on teachers and their teaching. For example, in Carlyon and Fisher's (2012) research, school leaders recognised the benefits of teachers experiencing teaching in different class levels and actively encouraged the change. The study on which this chapter is founded also identified a number of positive outcomes from this type of change. In line with previous research (Barnard & Ferrier-Kerr, 2021), however, the doctoral study findings also confirmed change and transition can pose mental and physical challenges for teachers as they attempt to maintain focus on their professional practice. Not surprising, the role of school leaders was highlighted in the study as being vital for teachers to successfully navigate change and transition. The actions of school leaders and their capacity to create a specific school culture that supports successful teacher change and transition emerged as being critical.

The role of school leaders

An integral aspect of a school leader's role is to cultivate and maintain a positive school culture that encompasses enhancing teaching and learning (Day et al., 2020). This was highlighted in the study, where teachers identified the essential role of school leaders to effectively facilitate the process of changing class levels, the transition process, and mitigate associated challenges. This was highlighted in survey responses from teachers which indicated that 80% ($n=387$) considered school leadership to have a substantial impact on their ability to navigate class-level changes. A representative comment echoed this sentiment: "It really depends on the school … the successful transition comes down to the leadership, school-wide culture, collegiality, communication".

It became evident from the study that school leaders played an integral role in establishing and sustaining a school culture in which teachers could successfully change class levels and navigate transition. When this occurred, the findings revealed that 86% (n=418) of teachers identified the change and transition as having a positive impact on their learning. Consistent with the work of Hargreaves and Fullan (2012), the study revealed a particular school culture was required to be established by school leaders for successful change and transition to occur. This school culture was characterised by relational trust, support, collaboration, and a common vision. Each of these aspects of a school culture is examined further in the subsequent sections.

Relational trust

Arguably, for teachers to benefit from opportunities for professional learning, it is essential for school leaders to build a school culture inclusive of relational trust with teachers (Anaru, 2018; Cranston, 2011). Findings from the study aligned with others who claim that relational trust is essential for a professional learning culture to develop in which teachers are willing to take risks (Cranston, 2011; du Plessis, 2013). Based on mutual accountability (Timperley et al., 2010), relational trust is developed when school leaders and teachers show integrity, honesty, and openness (Anaru, 2018).

Teachers conveyed a strong message that, to view change and transition positively, relational trust was needed for them to have confidence in their leader's decision making regarding the process of assigning teachers to class levels. Confirming earlier research (Carlyon, 2013), teachers emphasised the importance of their school leaders showing genuine commitment to understanding their individual needs as part of the process. For instance, as one teacher explained, "the principal at the time made the decision saying that it would give me a better grounding in the school—overall, getting to understand the culture and children better. He was right".

Effective communication and honest dialogue from school leaders, coupled with providing teachers with adequate time to prepare, facilitated positive perceptions of change and transition. This sentiment was reinforced by one teacher who stated, "I was allowed to make some errors along the way. It was all good for my professional development". Thus, when teachers felt that relational trust was established and that mistakes would not be criticised, they became more positive about change and transition.

Nevertheless, not all teachers reported having a high level of relational trust with their school leaders. There was evidence of school leaders failing to consider all necessary factors when managing change, signifying they considered the process to be a simple organisational task. Instances of poor communication and lack of consultation resulted in feelings of frustration, anger, loss of autonomy, and resistance to changing class levels. The following comment reflects this: "I was informed by email ... no discussion or options given. I felt shocked". These findings support Carlyon and Fisher's (2013) earlier assertion that, while a strategic approach to change is required, relational trust needs to be established first to overcome resistance.

Support

In alignment with Le Fevre's (2010) assertion that change "involves significant and complex issues at the individual, organisational and systemic levels" (p. 73), the study revealed that adequate and appropriate support was essential for teachers to navigate change and transition. Despite challenges, such as increased workload and perceptions held by others, teachers felt more confident about change and transition when supported by their school leaders. Support, both practical and emotional, was considered integral. As one teacher pointed out, "Change is full of uncertainties and initially quite daunting (especially jumping from Year 1 to Year 6)".

Examples of support for teachers included providing extra time to prepare, observing others teaching in different class levels, and accessing new resources. One teacher highlighted the value in having opportunities to prepare, stating, "This was hugely helpful ... I find that's how I learn best too, watching other people". Another teacher explained how the experience was positive when there was support: "In a learning school this change is the norm not the exception".

Mentoring relationships proves to be a valuable strategy, particularly in supporting teachers navigating through change and transition (Morrison & Ferrier-Kerr, 2015). School leaders play a pivotal role in setting up the infrastructure to support existing relationships and facilitate new ones. As reported in earlier research (Carlyon, 2014), mentors were found in the study to offer both practical and emotional support. They encouraged teachers to reflect on their practices, explore new ideas, and identify effective strategies for different class levels. Teachers emphasised the importance of having at least one person to rebound off, with one stating: "If she hadn't been there, I probably wouldn't have made the transition, and I don't think I would have handled the transition as well". The mentor's role was crucial in helping teachers navigate the change, gain confidence, and understand the transition process (Morrison & Ferrier-Kerr, 2015).

However, notwithstanding the support some teachers received, 39% (n=187) indicated they did not receive adequate support when they changed class levels. One participant summed this up by saying, "I have been subject to little but usually no time to prepare—always last minute and no lead-in time." Another teacher pointed out that "other people would have been watching a highly effective teacher of Years 5 and 6 go to Years 2/3 and actually not get a lot of support. I wonder what that does for encouraging other teachers to move class." Furthermore, instances were identified where a lack of understanding and consultation by school leaders resulted in some teachers receiving support that was neither appropriate nor helpful. One teacher highlighted the challenge of suddenly having a parent helper and teacher aide in the class to manage without prior experience, saying, "It would have actually been a lot easier just to be left for a little while by myself without them throwing all these people at me."

The teachers' experiences highlighted that when school leaders did not ensure adequate and appropriate support or consultation occurred, it resulted in teachers struggling to navigate the change and transition. The analogy of feeling left to "sink or swim" was used frequently by teachers. These findings bring to light the emotional labour that change and transition demand and support the argument of Newell et al. (2009) that it is impossible for teachers to "go it alone" (p. 107).

Collaboration

A school culture that is encouraging and supportive of collaboration is also essential for teachers to successfully negotiate change and transition (Carlyon, 2016b; Fisher & Carlyon, 2017). The study's findings were consistent with previous research (Day et al., 2020) emphasising the importance of school leaders building a school culture where collaboration is fostered. Hence, the benefits of teachers working collaboratively on the learning needs of all students are recognised (Hargreaves & Fullan, 2012).

When teachers were asked about the opportunities provided for collaboration before changing class levels, their experiences varied, with only 42% (n=205) responding positively. The opportunities for collaboration the teachers identified included sharing resources, observing others plan and teach, and engaging in conversations about changing class levels. One teacher expressed the value of collaboration, stating, "I've been in a really amazing team ... I could rely on others a lot in that first term to sort of collaborate with and get my head around things". School leaders played a crucial role in ensuring both formal and informal collaboration occurred. As one teacher pointed out, "When professional dialogue is encouraged, and time allocated for this, it is appreciated."

Despite the proven benefits of teachers working collaboratively, the study indicated that not all school leaders recognise this. There were reports of teachers having limited or no opportunities to collaborate with colleagues to prepare for their transition. For instance, as one teacher remarked, "I have never been given time to talk to other teachers within school time about the new level and what I need to know". Another teacher pointed out, "I would have very much liked the chance to observe in other Year 7/8 rooms to re-orientate myself."

The findings also brought to light that some school leaders may lack personal experience in changing class levels, leading to a limited understanding of the importance of collaboration. Confirming previous research (Carlyon & Fisher, 2012), teachers emphasised the value in school leaders gaining personal experience of teaching different class levels. This experience enriches their leadership practice and enhances their understanding of the importance of collaboration. Thus, it is essential for school leaders to cultivate a culture that encourages an understanding and practice of collaboration among and between teachers, to support the successful navigation of change and transition.

Common vision

Aligned with previous research, the study highlighted the significance of establishing and sharing a common vision to foster successful change within schools (Fennell, 2005; Meyer et al., 2023). A common vision, encompassing shared goals and beliefs, plays a fundamental role in cultivating a school culture where teachers are better positioned to achieve collective objectives. The study revealed that, when a common vision regarding changing class levels is shared, teachers gain a better understanding of its benefits, develop a collective responsibility for all students, and perceive the change and transition positively. Moreover, a common vision was shown to facilitate a smoother navigation of teachers' roles and the challenges associated with change events and the associated process of transition.

Teachers' responses indicated that when a common vision about change and transition was shared, they were able to understand the benefits more easily. One teacher observed, "I believe change is good, it keeps you energised, ensures self-learning, and keeps things fresh, rather than being stuck and uninspired". Additionally, 92% (n=445) of teachers reported that the change resulted in an increased sense of collective responsibility for all children, rather than just those in their class. A teacher elaborated, "I was not defined or confined to a particular year level or class; rather I saw my role as a teacher of all students, regardless of their age or developmental stage".

Furthermore, a common vision supports teachers to develop positive perceptions about change and transition. One teacher shared how the experience "made me a more reflective teacher and I now have a more inquiring approach to my teaching". Others talked about gaining a better understanding of student learning journeys, prompting adjustments to established teaching methods and the adoption of new practices designed to meet the diverse needs of students at various levels. A teacher reflected on how this influenced their practice, stating, "I now know what to do if they are 'stuck' at a stage as I have taught all stages and therefore have a wide range of tools to draw on, and it makes you more flexible in changing your practice, and makes you think of different ways to do things". These positive impacts on teachers' pedagogical practice are found to be unique to each teacher, collectively contributing to the strengthening of their professional identity and self-efficacy (Carlyon, 2016c). This was aptly described by one teacher as providing "a wide and rich tapestry to fall back on".

Despite the evident benefits, however, the study revealed that perceptions held by others posed a challenge for many teachers in the study, discouraging them from changing class levels. There was a shared belief among teachers that teaching higher class levels was often perceived as requiring more capable teachers, while changing to a lower level was sometimes stigmatised as a demotion. This perception highlighted the absence of a common vision in schools. An illustrative example was a teacher commenting that "a couple of parents who questioned me about moving to Years 7 and 8 once they heard I would be moving year groups. One parent seemed very surprised as if I surely wasn't capable after teaching Year 2 pupils." These findings bring to light the importance of establishing and sharing a common vison in schools. In addition, they confirm that it is incumbent upon school leaders to cultivate a school culture in which a common vision about change and transition is shared and teachers are better positioned to achieve collective objectives.

Conclusion

This chapter has drawn on findings primarily derived from the author's doctoral research which focused on teacher change and transition between class levels in primary schools and the impact of this upon their teacher professional learning. This and earlier studies (Carlyon, 2011; Carlyon & Fisher, 2012; Fisher & Carlyon, 2017) also explored the role of school leadership in the process of teacher change and transition. Despite the time that has passed since the study, there remains a lack of literature. This would appear to indicate that this specific practice has been, and continues to be, under-researched and sometimes overlooked as an opportunity for teachers to undergo a unique and enriching form of professional learning tailored to their individual needs and contexts. Notably, it could be professional learning that has the potential to improve their pedagogical practice.

There can be no denying the significant benefits for teachers and teaching when change and transition are effectively facilitated. However, the process is heavily dependent on the actions of school leaders. Change and the process of transition can tend to be challenging for teachers and require school leaders to have the knowledge and skills to facilitate both effectively. School leaders should be mindful that, although the transition between class levels is an observable process, the transition occurring for teachers internally—as they navigate the change—is less observable.

Relational trust between teachers and school leaders is essential, as is ensuring teachers have support and opportunities to work collaboratively with others. Most importantly, it is essential school leaders establish and share a common vision regarding change and transition in schools to facilitate a smooth navigation of teachers' roles and the challenges.

The actions taken by school leaders and their capacity to cultivate a specific school culture, wherein teachers feel a sense of autonomy and are adept at navigating change and transition, are crucial. The specific school culture required for successful change and transition in schools is characterised by relational trust, support, collaboration, and a common vision. It is imperative that school leaders know how to create this school culture to support teacher change and transition, in particular between class levels, for teacher professional learning.

References

Anaru, L. (2018). *Building relational trust*. Ministry of Education. https://www.educationalleaders.govt.nz/Leadership-development/Professional-information/Leadership-capability-framework/High-trust-relationships/Building-relational-trust

Barker, M. (2023). When tomorrow comes: Contextualising the independent review of Tomorrow's Schools. *Policy Quarterly*, *19*(3), 11–18. https://doi.org/10.26686/pq.v19i3.8307

Berryman, M., Ford, T., & Egan, M. (2015). Developing collaborative connections between schools and Māori communities. *Set: Research Information for Teachers*, (3), 18–25. https://doi.org/10.18296/set.0023

Branson, C. M., Marra, M., & Kidson, K. (2024). Responding to the current capricious state of Australian educational leadership: We should have seen it coming! *Education Sciences*, *4*, 410. https://doi.org/10.3390/educsci14040410

Constantinides, M. (2023). Successful school leadership in New Zealand: A scoping review. *Education Sciences*, *13*(12), 1189. https://doi.org/10.3390/educsci13121189)

Day, C., Gorgen, K., & Sammons, P. (2020). *Successful school leadership*. Education Development Trust. https://www.edt.org/research-and-insights/successful-school-leadership-2020-publication/

Dharan, V., Pond, R., & Mincher, N. (2022). *Teacher and student well-being in the Covid-19 pandemic*. Massey University. https://mro.massey.ac.nz/server/api/core/bitstreams/f40cd6e6-6b73-4740-b962-d17b7ef992e4/content

Education Council New Zealand . (2018). *Educational Leadership Capability Framework*. https://teachingcouncil.nz/assets/Files/Leadership-Strategy/Leadership_Capability_Framework.pdf

Fisher, A., & Carlyon, T. (2014). School leaders growing leadership from within: A framework for the development of school leaders. *Waikato Journal of Education*, *19*(2), 93–102. https://doi.org/10.15663/wje.v20i2.179

Fullan, M. (2003). *The moral imperative of school leadership*. SAGE Publications.

Jagger, D. (2020). *School principals in New Zealand*. Ministry of Education. https://www.educationcounts.govt.nz/publications/schooling2/workforce

Jones, L. (2022). Why many school principals are CEOs, in principle. *School principal or CEO?* Fisher Leadership. https://fisherleadership.com/school-principal-or-ceo/

Le Fevre, D. (2010). Changing tack: Talking about change knowledge for professional learning. In H. Timperley & J. Parr (Eds.), *Weaving evidence, inquiry and standards to build better schools* (pp. 71–92). NZCER Press.

Macann, G. (2020). Leadership in our secondary schools: Good people, inadequate systems. *Journal of Educational Leadership, Policy and Practice*, *35*(Special Issue), 14–24. https://doi.org/10.21307/jelpp-2020-004

Ministry of Education. (2008). *Kiwi leadership for principals*. https://www.educationalleaders.govt.nz/Leadership-development/Key-leadership-documents/Kiwi-leadership-for-principals

Ministry of Education. (2010). *Tū rangatira Māori medium educational leadership*. https://www.educationalleaders.govt.nz/Leadership-development/Key-leadership-documents/Tu-rangatira-English

Ministry of Education. (2020). *The statement of national education and learning priorities (NELP)*. https://assets.education.govt.nz/public/Documents/NELP-TES-documents/FULL-NELP-2020.pdf

Notman, R. (2020). An evolution in distributed educational leadership: From sole leader to co-principalship. *Journal of Educational Leadership, Policy and Practice, 35*(Special Issue), 27–40. https://doi.org/10.21307/jelpp-2020-005

Notman, R., & Henry, D. A. (2009). The human face of principalship: A synthesis of case study findings. *Journal of Educational Leadership, Policy and Practice, 24*(1), 37–52. https://search.informit.org/doi/pdf/10.3316/informit.872314902981261

Notman, R., & Henry, D. A. (2011). Building and sustaining successful school leadership in New Zealand. *Leadership and Policy in Schools, 10*, 375–394. https://doi.org/10.1080/15700763.2011.610555

Ranjan, R. (2024, January 4). *How can you manage unrealistic expectations from parents?* Linkedin. https://www.linkedin.com/pulse/how-can-you-manage-unrealistic-expectations-from-parents-ranjan-aoakf

Robinson, V., & Gray, E. (2019). What difference does school leadership make to student outcomes? *Journal of the Royal Society of New Zealand, 49*(2), 171–187. https://doi.org/10.1080/03036758.2019.1582075

Robinson, V., Hohepa, M., & Lloyd, C. (2009). *School leadership and student outcomes: Identifying what works and why: Best Evidence Synthesis iteration (BES)*. Ministry of Education. https://www.educationcounts.govt.nz/publications/series/2515/60170

Starr, J. P. (2022). Expectations and exceptions on leadership. *Kappan, 104*(4), 60–61. https://doi.org/10.1177/00317217221142988

Stoll, L. (2000). School culture. *Set: Research Information for Teachers*, (3), 9–14. https://doi.org/10.18296/set.0805

Thrupp, M. (2007). Education's "inconvenient truth": Persistent middle class advantage. [An inaugural professorial lecture]. *Waikato Journal of Education, 13*, 253–271. https://researchcommons.waikato.ac.nz/server/api/core/bitstreams/df4031b7-74dc-4409-9494-971c01a990e9/content

Thrupp, M. (2023). Education's "inconvenient truth": Part two—The middle classes have too many friends in education. *New Zealand Journal of Teachers' Work, 20*(1), 117–125. https://doi.org/10.24135/teacherswork.v20i1.441

Tomorrow's Schools Independent Taskforce. (2018). *Our schooling futures: Stronger together*. Ministry of Education. https://conversation.education.govt.nz/assets/TSR/Tomorrows-Schools-Review-Report-13Dec2018.PDF

Upsall, D. (2004). Shared principalship of schools. *New Zealand Annual Review of Education, 13*, 143–168. https://doi.org/10.26686/nzaroe.v0i13.1452

Wylie, C. (2020). What does it mean to be a principal? A policy researcher's perspective on the last 30 years in Aotearoa New Zealand. *Journal of Educational Leadership, Policy and Practice, 35*(Special Issue), 41–58. https://doi.org/10.21307/jelpp-2020-007

Youngs, H. (2020). Thirty years of leadership in New Zealand education: From the shadows of management to sine qua non. *Journal of Educational Leadership, Policy and Practice, 35*(Special Issue), 59–77. https://doi.org/10.21307/jelpp-2020-008

Chapter 11

Middle leadership in primary schools in Aotearoa New Zealand

Richard Edwards

Introduction

Leadership in education has a long and rich heritage of research and thinking (Rönnerman et al., 2017). The unit of focus is typically the school and the key people involved in leading the school—in other words, the principal or head teacher and the senior management or leadership team. While greater emphasis has been given to leadership in secondary schools, there is also considerable research that focuses on primary schools. The area of middle leadership in primary schools, however, remains underrepresented in the literature (De Nobile, 2018), yet it plays a vital role in both the direction and operation of the school.

In New Zealand primary schools, middle leadership is acknowledged as integral to the effective functioning of a school (Cardno et al., 2018; Ministry of Education, 2012). A significant driver in the development of middle leadership in New Zealand schools, particularly primary schools, came with the Tomorrow's Schools policy shift from centralised regional decision making to school-based management and decision making (Bassett & Shaw, 2018; Cardno, 2012). Prior to this, teachers had limited direct involvement in the management of primary schools. Growing recognition of the role of middle leadership in the effective functioning of schools has contributed to an increase in research and theorising in this area.

This chapter explores the often-overlooked area of middle leadership in primary schools. The content of the chapter is primarily drawn from a review of recent literature. While a broad perspective is taken, the emphasis is on understanding middle leadership in the context of Aotearoa New Zealand primary schools. The chapter starts with a discussion of the nature of middle leadership in primary schools before exploring what middle leaders do and how their practice is consistent with recent theoretical models. The next section explores who middle leaders are. This is followed by a vignette of one middle leader to add a personal dimension to the discussion, and a conclusion.

Middle leadership in education

A growing appreciation of the role and importance of middle leadership has been reflected in a significant increase in research and publication over the past two decades (De Nobile, 2021; Harris et al, 2019). Alongside this, De Nobile (2018) notes a shift in focus from middle management to middle leadership. He attributes this to greater recognition of the evolution of the roles undertaken in these positions, from administrative and managerial tasks to more strategic and learning-oriented tasks. However, recent reviews in the field (De Nobile, 2021; Harris et al., 2019; Lipscombe et al., 2023) indicate that, in comparison with other areas of educational leadership, middle leadership is under-researched and under-theorised.

One of the challenges is that the concept of middle leadership is complex and hard to define (Lipscombe et al., 2020). Leadership that is exercised in the space between the senior leadership team and the classroom teacher could be described as middle leadership. In that sense, it is indeed in the middle. However, the idea of the middle can be seen as somehow mediocre or average, or as primarily about connecting two ends. From this point of view, it seems neither interesting nor particularly important. Hargreaves (2024), in contrast, discusses the concept of the middle, noting that it should be seen as the "the beating heart of everything we are trying to accomplish together" (p. xvii). Its "betweenness" belies the importance of middle leadership in providing direction and resilience in school operations.

A useful definition of a middle leader is that they have the dual role of providing leadership in a school while maintaining regular teaching commitments (Gear & Sood, 2021; Grootenboer, Tindall-Ford, et al.,

2023; Tindall-Ford et al., 2024). Alongside this Grootenboer, Tindall-Ford, et al. (2023) identify three characteristics of middle leading that further clarify the middle leadership role:
- Positional—middle leaders sit between senior leadership and the teaching staff with involvement in both groups.
- Philosophical—the leadership exercised by middle leaders is typically alongside their colleagues and is collaborative rather than directive.
- Practical—middle leadership is a practice with its own character and needs to be understood in terms of its "sayings, doings, and relatings". (p. 456)

While this definition may seem simple, it is made complex by the wide diversity of roles and situations that middle leaders may occupy. In addition, middle leadership roles are identified by a plethora of titles (Farchi & Tubin, 2019) that vary depending on the nature of the school, the education system in which they operate, and the local and national context. A more constrained definition used by Lipscombe et al. (2023) in their recent review of the literature identifies middle leadership as involving a formal position and accountability for designated responsibilities. They emphasise the leadership aspect of the role and make a distinction from teacher leadership. Most authors would agree that middle leadership and teacher leadership are not the same. The role of a teacher is very much that of a leader, primarily expressed through leading learning within their own classrooms and supporting exemplary practice with colleagues. However, not all people involved in middle leadership have formal positions, and the degree of accountability can be quite low. It may therefore be better to view middle leadership as a range. What defines middle leadership in schools then is that it operates between senior leadership and teachers, involves leadership of specific aspects of school life, and has a strong teaching and learning orientation.

One of the reasons middle leadership is complex is the enormous diversity of contexts within which it occurs. The theory of practice architectures has been used to describe and understand middle leadership contexts (Rönnerman et al., 2017). It views middle leadership as a practice involving saying, doing, and relating and identifies three sets of "arrangements" that both make the practice possible and hold it in place. They are:

- Cultural–discursive arrangements—mediated through language; these make the "sayings" of the practice possible.
- Material–economic arrangements—mediated through physical objects, space, and time; these make the "doings" of the practice possible.
- Social–political arrangements—mediated through power, solidarity, and agency; these make the "relatings" of the practice possible.

Hargreaves (2024) suggests that leading from the middle requires three things: a philosophy of inclusion that inspires everyone; a culture of norms, beliefs, and habits that guide them; and a structure of time, space, roles, and responsibilities that supports them. Middle leadership is therefore very much dependent on the context within which it is operating and is very much a situated practice.

The following section explores current thinking, particularly from the perspective of middle leadership as a practice and in answer to the question, "What do middle leaders do?"

What do middle leaders do?

The role of middle leadership has been described in a number of ways. Based on an extensive review of the literature, De Nobile (2018, 2019, 2021) developed the Middle Leadership in Schools (MLiS) Model (Figure 11.1) to guide theorising and research.

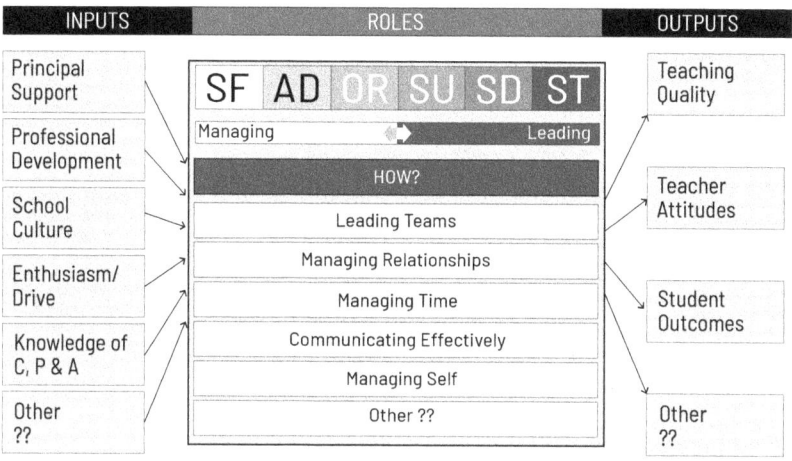

Figure 11.1 The MLiS Model, from De Nobile (2021, p. 6)

The model identifies six roles (initials across the top of the middle box) by which a middle leader responds to a range of inputs to influence a range of specific outcomes:

- Student-focused role (SF)—dealing directly with students and their issues
- Administrative (AD)—developing procedures and systems and maintaining them
- Organisational role (OR)—primarily about organising people
- Supervisory role (SU)—monitoring and evaluating staff performance
- Staff development role (SD)—supporting teachers with coaching, mentoring, or other direct assistance; also leading by example
- Strategic role (ST)—setting goals and developing visions for their area of responsibility.

Each role is enacted through careful balancing and management of time commitments, relationships, emotions, and other aspects of self, and through effective communication and a collaborative approach. Each middle leader is involved in the roles above to different extents, even though not all roles are part of what some middle leaders do.

The model highlights how important the quality of input (left side of model) is in enabling middle leaders to carry out their role. For example, the role of the principal is crucial in terms of both their relationship with the middle leader and their support for what the middle leader does (Bassett & Shaw, 2018; Farchi & Tubin, 2019). Also, a number of studies have noted a need for more professional learning opportunities for middle leaders, citing frequent expressions of a lack of confidence by middle leaders (Bassett & Shaw, 2018; Grootenboer, Tindall-Ford, et al., 2023). While many middle leaders have expertise and experience in the area in which they are leading and in teaching, they don't necessarily have leadership expertise and experience (Gear & Sood, 2021; Grootenboer & Edwards-Groves, 2020). In fact, many middle leaders see themselves primarily as teachers rather than leaders (Bassett & Shaw, 2018). The model also highlights the areas in which middle leadership has an impact. In general, there is agreement that middle leadership has an impact on teaching quality, teacher attitudes, and student outcomes, but there is little research that focuses on this and it has been identified as an area of need (De Nobile, 2021; Harris et al., 2019; Lipscombe et al., 2023).

A second more recent model (Tindall-Ford et al., 2024) focused more specifically on middle leadership practices. Their research led them to identify four practices that characterise middle leadership. This, too, was intended to provide a starting point for future research:
- Leading and managing school teaching, learning, and curriculum
- Supporting teacher colleagues' development
- Collaborating with teacher colleagues on teaching and learning
- Collaborating with, and advocating to, the school principal.

This model highlights more clearly the relational, supportive, and collaborative nature of middle leadership. The model also acknowledges the dynamic and responsive nature of middle leadership. Regardless of the model, however, middle leadership is essentially a human endeavour. This is the focus of the next section.

Who is the middle leader?

Each person in the role of a middle leader brings a rich and unique array of knowledge, skills, and experience to the role. It is often this that is the catalyst for their involvement in middle leadership. In primary schools, many teachers take on some form of leadership because of the complex array of areas in which leadership is needed and the limited pool of people who can provide that leadership. Primary schools in particular rely heavily on their staff to provide that leadership at a middle leader level. In this sense, the leadership can be seen as distributed, despite some research suggesting that context at times prevents middle leadership practice from matching distributed leadership (Hammersley-Fletcher & Kirkham, 2007; Lárusdóttir & O'Connor, 2017).

Middle leaders emerge in a variety of ways and with a variety of aspirations and motivations. Kerry (2021) suggests teachers become middle leaders by taking on a temporary role when someone is away, volunteering, being identified as particularly capable, or simply seeking a new challenge. Grootenboer, Attard, et al. (2023) describe pathways into middle leadership in a similar way as being by "accident, aspiration, or being anointed" (p. 45). This suggests that a desire to make use of their areas of expertise and an interest in improving teaching and learning are often more important motivations than a desire to become a leader. For some, however, middle leadership is seen as a stepping stone to senior leadership (Marshall, 2022), although Grootenboer et al. (2021) dispute this, suggesting that middle leaders are not just principals-in-waiting. They argue that middle leaders are "uniquely and critically positioned to lead curriculum and pedagogical development in schools" (p. 43), and that we need to better understand middle leadership and the support it requires to be effective.

The following vignette provides an example of a teacher involved in middle leadership. It is intended to offer a more personal perspective on what is discussed above.

Vignette of a middle leader

This vignette puts a human "face" on middle leadership by presenting some key experiences and reflections of a teacher in a New Zealand primary school as expressed in an interview. It is anonymised to both protect the identity of the teacher and reflect similarities to the experience of many other teachers involved in middle leadership. The teacher's voice is used where possible, and their experience is linked to key points raised earlier.

The teacher, whose name for this vignette is Eric, trained in a typical Initial Teacher Education Graduate Diploma programme at a New Zealand university, having first completed a science degree. Since then, he had been teaching for 10 years at a suburban primary school in a large urban centre in Aotearoa New Zealand. He was identified by his principal as someone at his school who had an interest and experience in teaching and leading science, technology, engineering, and maths (STEM) education.

Around 5 years ago, Eric's school was accepted into a government-funded whole-school science teaching development opportunity administered by the Royal Society Te Apārangi. Because of his interest and background in science, Eric was chosen to undertake the professional learning that he would then feed back into the development of science programmes at his school:

> I did the science teaching leadership programme and learned about teaching science through the nature of science primarily. Then we worked in an onsite science experience with each six months in a different organisation, ... where I worked alongside their scientists doing whichever projects, ...

Of particular note here is that Eric was not seeking middle leadership responsibilities. However, he was willing to take advantage of the opportunity when it was offered because of his interest and background in science. Interestingly, the programme he and his school were applying for was a relatively rare example of a programme specifically designed to support the development and practice of middle leadership in New Zealand schools. On his return to his school, Eric was involved in ongoing development of the school's science teaching capability:

> Then I came back and helped to devise a science curriculum for school. So we went with using a science capability[1] as the focus for

---

1   For a discussion of the science capabilities, see Hipkins and Bull (2015).

the year ... Then at the same time we have a content focus ... Every year, we teach the teachers how to teach by asking questions of the capabilities.

Here Eric shows evidence of three of the four middle leadership practices identified by Tindall-Ford et al. (2024)—leading and managing school teaching, learning, and curriculum; supporting teacher colleagues' development; and collaborating with teacher colleagues on teaching and learning. He had direct input into curriculum planning, teacher development, and developing resources. Eric is notably consistent in his use of the term "we" when referring to what he was doing, implying an emphasis on collaboration and communication. However, the two defining characteristics of middle leaders (appointment to a specific position and having accountable responsibilities) that Lipscombe et al. (2023) identified in their review of the literature were not part of Eric's middle leadership experience. While the science teaching leadership programme came with the expectation that participants would provide leadership in the science learning area, in Eric's case this was not a specified position and there were no staff reporting to him. In spite of this, though, it is clear that Eric is engaged in middle leadership.

Eric was also involved in weaving technology, engineering, and maths into his work supporting the development of teaching and curriculum at his school. He admitted knowing less about these areas:

> Yeah, I don't have knowledge of that really. I mostly have knowledge of science and then just building and creating, but not really ... I mean, engineering—it's the building part, right? Whereas the tech might be the design and the process as well as the outcome. But yeah, I feel I have less understanding of that.

However, this didn't diminish his confidence in what he was doing. Rather, he accommodated it through focusing on what he did know and on a more general emphasis on enabling students to pursue their own interests. He also placed a high degree of trust in a range of STEM-oriented programmes that had been promoted to the school and that the school had bought into, although he wasn't often involved in the decision making about their adoption. This was more often driven by individual teachers and their interests.

Eric identified a range of factors he saw as being supportive of performing his middle leadership role. The most important was the support of his principal. The support came in the form of the principal having confidence in Eric's knowledge and skills and trusting him to provide the leadership in the particular area that the school needed. It was practical in the provision of time, opportunities to work with staff, and funding for resources. It was also important to Eric that he had the confidence of the staff with whom he was working. Eric spoke of his experience in this role in a very natural way and it was clear that he saw his role as contributing to the work of a team rather than leading from the front. He clearly benefited from the targeted professional development he received at the start. He was also developing a strong set of knowledge and skills that he could use in his role as it continued and that set him up for other leadership roles in the future.

Conclusion

It is clear that middle leadership is a rich and important contributor to the effective operation of primary schools. It is also clear that recognition of this leadership is a relatively recent phenomenon and that middle leadership is currently a growing field of research and theorising. The complexity of middle leadership is heightened by the diversity of contexts within which it operates, yet we are becoming clearer about the practices that comprise middle leadership and how it differs from senior leadership. Appreciating middle leadership from the perspective of the person who leads in the middle is also key to understanding its effectiveness in primary schools.

Middle leadership in primary schools in Aotearoa New Zealand has many similarities to that described in other countries (Fitzgerald & Gunter, 2006; Gurr, 2019) although the importance of context means that there are some distinctly New Zealand "flavours" to it (Highfield, 2017). These include an emphasis on school-based curriculum development, Aotearoa New Zealand's bicultural identity as a nation, and a strong commitment to inclusion. However, these are rather under-researched and there is clearly scope for research to provide valuable insights to guide future policy, school practice, and the professional learning of our future middle leaders.

References

Bassett, M., & Shaw, N. (2018). Building the confidence of first-time middle leaders in New Zealand primary schools. *International Journal of Educational Management, 32*(5), 749–760. https://doi.org/10.1108/IJEM-05-2017-0101

Cardno, C. (2012). *Managing effective relationships in education.* SAGE Publications.

Cardno, C., Robson, J., Deo, A., Bassett M., & Howse, J. (2018). Middle-level leaders as direct instructional leaders in New Zealand schools: A study of role expectations and performance confidence. *Journal of Educational Leadership, Policy and Practice, 33*(2), 32–47. https://doi.org/10.21307/jelpp-2018-011

De Nobile, J. (2018). Towards a theoretical model of middle leadership in schools. *School Leadership and Management, 38*(4), 395–416. https://doi.org/10.1080/13632434.2017.1411902

De Nobile, J. (2019). The roles of middle leaders in schools: Developing a conceptual framework for research. *Leading & Managing, 25*(1), 1–14.

De Nobile, J. (2021). Researching middle leadership in schools: The state of the art. *International Studies in Educational Administration, 49*, 3-27.

Farchi, T., & Tubin, D. (2019). Middle leaders in successful and less successful schools. *School Leadership & Management, 39*(3–4), 372–390. https://doi.org/10.1080/13632434.2018.1550389

Fitzgerald, T., & Gunter, H. (2006). Leading learning: Middle leadership in schools in England and New Zealand. *Management in Education, 20*(3), 6–8. https://doi.org/10.1177/08920206060200030201

Gear, R. C., & Sood, K. K. (2021). School middle leaders and change management: Do they need to be more on the "balcony" than the dance floor? *Education Sciences, 11*, 753. https://doi.org/10.3390/educsci11110753

Grootenboer, P., Attard, C., Edwards-Groves, C. J., Tindall-Ford, S., & Ahern, S. (2023). Becoming a middle leader: Accidental, aspirational, or anointed. *Leading & Managing, 29*(1), 43–50.

Grootenboer, P., & Edwards-Groves, C. (2020). Educational middle leading: A critical practice in school development. *Leading & Managing, 26*(1), 25–30.

Grootenboer, P., Edwards-Groves, C., Attard, C., & Tindall-Ford, S. (2021) Middle leaders are not just principals-in-waiting. *Australian Educational Leader, 43*, 41–43.

Grootenboer, P., Tindall-Ford, S., Edwards-Groves, C., & Attard, C. (2023) Establishing an evidence-base for supporting middle leadership practice development in schools. *School Leadership & Management, 43*(5), 454–472. https://doi.org/10.1080/13632434.2023.2271957

Gurr, D. (2019). School middle leaders in Australia, Chile and Singapore. *School Leadership & Management, 39*(3-4), 278-296. https://doi.org/10.1080/13632434.2018.1512485

Hammersley-Fletcher, L., & Kirkham, G. (2007). Middle leadership in primary school communities of practice: Distribution or deception? *School Leadership & Management, 27*(5), 423-443. http://dx.doi.org/10.1080/13632430701606087

Hargreaves, A. (2024). *Leadership from the middle: The beating heart of educational transformation.* Routledge.

Harris, A., Jones, M., Ismail, N., & Nguyen, D. (2019). Middle leaders and middle leadership in schools: Exploring the knowledge base (2003-2017). *School Leadership & Management, 39*(3-4), 255-277. https://doi.org/10.1080/13632434.2019.1578738

Highfield, C. (2017). *Middle leadership: The possibilities and potential.* Summary paper. Education Council New Zealand.

Hipkins, R., & Bull, A. (2015). Science capabilities for a functional understanding of the nature of science. *Curriculum Matters, 11*, 117-133. http://dx.doi.org/10.18296/cm.0007

Kerry, T. (2021). *Stand up and be counted: Middle leadership in education contexts.* Routledge.

Lárusdóttir, S. H., & O'Connor, E. (2017). Distributed leadership and middle leadership practice in schools: A disconnect? *Irish Educational Studies, 36*(4), 423-438. https://doi.org/10.1080/03323315.2017.1333444

Lipscombe, K., Grice, C., Tindall-Ford, S., & De-Nobile, J. (2020). Middle leading in Australian schools: Professional standards, positions, and professional development. *School Leadership & Management, 40*(5), 406-424. http://dx.doi.org/10.1080/13632434.2020.1731685

Lipscombe, K., Tindall-Ford, S., & Lamanna, J. (2023). School middle leadership: A systematic review. *Educational Management, Administration, and Leadership, 51*(2), 270-288.

Marshall, I. (2022). *The early years of leadership: The journey begins.* Information Age Publishing.

Ministry of Education. (2012). *Leading from the middle: Educational leadership for middle and senior leaders.* Learning Media. https://www.educationalleaders.govt.nz/Leadership-development/Key-leadership-documents/Leading-from-the-middle

Rönnerman, K., Grootenboer, P., & Edwards-Groves, C. (2017). The practice architectures of middle leading in early childhood education. *International Journal of Child Care and Education Policy, 11*(8), 1-20. http://dx.doi.org/10.1186/s40723-017-0032-z

Tindall-Ford, S., Grootenboer, P., Edwards-Groves, C., & Attard, C. (2024). Understanding school middle-leading practices: Developing a middle-leading practice model. *Education Sciences, 14*, 492. http://dx.doi.org/10.3390/educsci14050492

Chapter 12
Relational leadership: Teachers' perceptions of leaders' behaviours and actions

Anthony Fisher

Introduction

The importance of relationships has not always been recognised in leadership theory. In an investigation of a range of leaders by Daly (2010) across several contexts, it was noted that, although the contexts varied and involved different members, one aspect was always present. That was the importance of relationships. This highlights that it is the relational links between participants, within their context, that are important to leadership. These relational links are often taken for granted, despite being referred to as being important and are often reduced to an "objectified casual transaction" (Giles, 2019, p. 5). However, placing a greater importance on the role relationships have as being central to education is recognised by Giles et al. (2012, p. 215) who said: "Relationships are at the heart of educational encounters." Therefore, the relational aspect can be understood as the essence of leadership, as the interactions between leaders and those in their context are critical.

In the context of leading a primary school, it is relationships that allow principals as leaders to bring about change, be innovative, and meet the ever-changing demands of their complex roles. The complexity of the role of a primary school principal has led to a proliferation of leadership research and the identification of leadership styles. Despite this, much of the research has tended to focus on management, administration, and meeting standards, etc., which is not a comprehensive understanding of leadership. What is missing is not more information in relation to style or traits but, as identified by Timperley and Hulsbosch (2010), "We need fewer reports about leadership and more analysis of leadership in action" (p. 1). This notion that there is more to leadership than just style is also put forward by Haslam et al. (2011) who identified that, despite the emphasis remaining on characteristics of leaders, leadership is not about leaders alone. Leadership is very much about the interpersonal relationships and connections leaders have in order to lead.

This chapter discusses ways in which these interpersonal relationships develop, disclosing teachers' perspectives on building relationships with principals. It explains the importance of knowing the principal informally before developing a professional relationship, the need for the principal to be present, and the importance of informal encounters between teacher and principal. The data presented in this chapter are taken from a research project that aimed to gain a greater understanding of what teachers perceive as important to establishing and growing a relationship with their principal. Additionally, the research aimed to provide an insight into the actions principals display that help to facilitate these connections and promote relational growth and development. This chapter first provides a brief outline of the details of the study on which the chapter is based, followed by an overview of the literature. Then the findings from the research are presented under the following three themes: knowing the principal informally before developing a professional relationship; being present; and informal encounters. And finally, this is followed by a conclusion.

The study

The data for this chapter are taken from part of a larger study that aimed to inquire into the phenomena of social networks within a school setting and the relationship between teachers and principals. The study adopted a case study approach based on three premises as theorised by Blumer (1969). The first premise is centred on the understanding that humans' actions towards people, objects, or situations are based on meanings they have constructed. The second premise attributes meaning to social interaction with others. The third premise is that these meanings are understood and developed via a process of interpretation by the researcher.

Twelve teachers from three schools within three regions of Aotearoa New Zealand—South Auckland, Waikato, and Bay of Plenty—were included. Each participant was invited to take part in a semistructured individual interview to elicit qualitative data relevant to their experiences and perceptions of their relationship with the principal and their observations of leadership in action.

Relational leadership styles

As times are changing, the challenges faced by leaders are enormous. One of the biggest challenges is to make people and organisations adaptable and resilient, as identified by Maritsa et. al. (2022). This ability to be adaptable and resilient requires relationships that allow change to occur. Arguably then, the most important learning for a school principal is that of being able to work productively and co-operatively with others. Today, the school principal is expected to work closely with others, not in isolation from others, in establishing and achieving the educational outcomes desired by the school community. Principals being expected to work closely with others calls for a relational approach to school leadership. Thus, it is critical that principals understand teachers' perspective on how relationships develop if they want to build a relational approach to their leadership.

To understand the relationships between principals and teachers, as Timperley and Hulsbosch (2010) have said previously, there needs to be a call for more research into leadership in action. Two styles—authentic and trans-relational leadership, which will be discussed next—appear to be central to developing and maintaining relationships between principals and teachers, and are key to understanding the ways in which interpersonal relationships between teachers and their principal develop.

Authentic leadership

Authentic leadership has arisen from ethical and moral leadership. This style of leadership focuses on personality traits such as self-awareness, transparency, and ethics (Avolio et al., 2004) which informs the leaders' actions and how they are perceived. It is characterised by leaders engaging in honest dialogue which enables them to get to know their teachers as individuals (Begley, 2006) and for teachers to get to know them as well. Therefore, authentic leadership can be defined as leaders who have a clear sense of purpose, who practise enduring values such as integrity, lead with the heart, establish lasting, stable relationships, and demonstrate self-discipline. This type of leadership can be considered as taking a strength-based approach to leadership (Caza & Jackson, 2011). However, there are some drawbacks. Caza and Jackson (2011) identified the following two points as being drawbacks to authentic leadership: firstly, there is an embedded belief that authentic leadership is totally desirable as a way of leading; and secondly, there is a similar belief that it only produces positive outcomes. What this is saying is that having a rigid authenticity may not fit all situations and at times it may be inappropriate to disclose everything you feel or think.

Trans-relational leadership

The second leadership style to be discussed is trans-relational leadership which provides a far greater emphasis on the importance of building supportive relationships. The central premise of trans-relational leadership is "to move others, the organisation and the leader to another level of functioning by means of relationships" as identified by Branson et al. (2018, p. 49). Further to this notion of moving people forward by a relational approach, Wheatley (2006) identified the need for principals to continually develop and maintain the relationship they have with their teachers and their practice and pedagogy. For teachers to continue to grow and develop, a trans-relational leader is required to create a culture that enables teachers to be motivated to achieve their best and is safe (Branson et al., 2016).

This understanding of the importance of relationships for principals was emphasised as early as 2008 by the Ministry of Education in their publication, *Kiwi Leadership for Principals*. In this publication, the Ministry of Education identified that, for principals to meet the challenges of principalship in the 21st century, it was important for principals to develop a climate of mutually trusting relationships. Furthermore, it could be considered it is the role of the principal to develop the conditions that foster a sense of them as the leader and as being trustworthy (Branson & Marra, 2019). This earning of leadership is often seen in the way principals support and facilitate reciprocal relationships (Branson et al., 2018). The development of these relationships sits within the everyday interactions that principals have with their teachers (Crevani et al., 2010).

Everyday interactions set the climate that is necessary to foster development and to meet the changing needs of their role as a leader of learning within schools. This understanding of the importance of relationships has been further identified by Timperley et al. (2020) in that the role of principal is complex and requires the principal to interact with others, thereby creating interdependencies based on the relationships formed.

Teachers' perspectives on building relationships with their principals

Three key ideas were identified when analysing the data regarding what teachers in the study perceived as being important aspects of building relationships with their principals.

- knowing the principal informally before developing a professional relationship
- being present
- informal encounters.

Findings from the study are discussed next under these key ideas.

Knowing the principal informally before developing a professional relationship

For the teachers in the study, knowing the principal as a person prior to developing a professional relationship was important. As Teacher A explained:

> If he's going to be my boss and he's going to make decisions and he's going to run our school, as a human being I want to know what sort of person he is. I want to know what sort of person you are as a human being.

Many of the teachers perceived that having this knowledge of who the principal was as a person was a way of making connections. Developing such important connections can only be done via the establishment of a mutually acceptable relationship as identified by Branson and Marra (2019). How these important connections and relationships were developed was explained by Teacher B as:

> making connections with your life ... he knows I've done a lot of travel, so he asks me about it. He asks about my husband, he asks about my house, what's going on without intruding on my private life.

These findings align with other research that highlighted the importance of principals having a clear understanding of who their teachers are (Begley, 2006). As Teacher B explained, the principal needed to know them and understand them as a person before they could know them as a professional:

> I'm doing my job; you trust the person I am. You know my values; you know where I come from and if you don't know that about me then how are you meant to know who I am as a professional?

However, despite the teachers wanting to know the principal as a person, most placed the onus on the principal to develop personal relationships. For the principal to be thought of by teachers as authentic, Frankham et al. (2018) suggested that leaders needed to take a more faciliatory approach over time. For the principal to be seen as facilitating the development of these relationships, the teachers considered it was important for the principal to take the lead in sharing who they were. Teacher B highlighted this when she said, "You can't just expect your staff to share everything with you and be a closed book." Although some teachers expected the principal to take the lead in sharing personal information, others saw it as a two-way process where the amount of personal content and the detail shared by the teachers was determined by the principal's willingness to share information about themselves. The teachers also identified that there were boundaries around sharing about who they were. For most of the teachers, the more personal aspects of their life went beyond what they would share with their principal. This finding was evident as eight of the 12 teachers interviewed stated they preferred to keep their personal life separate from their professional/school life.

Knowing the principal on a personal/informal level enabled the teachers to know the principal as a person and to make connections that helped to foster the relationship between them. Branson and Marra (2019) have also discussed the importance of leaders knowing who they are leading. In this research, a similar sentiment was expressed by the teachers; they needed to know who the principal was. Making these connections was critical, and was about knowing the principal as a person first, before seeing them as the professional leader. Teacher A expressed it as: "If you know the person, then you will know if they are being authentic or not in their professional life." For the teachers, making these authentic connections was also about aligning their own values and beliefs with those of the principal, which enabled them to develop trust in their principal.

For all the teachers, knowing the person was also seen as knowing that the principal was authentic. The importance of seeing their principal as being an authentic person and leader was a strong finding that emerged from the data. Teacher C explained: "It was important for the principal to be seen as the 'real' person they always are and [having] strong morals and a strong character".

Developing trust for the teachers was perceived as being important for the development of an authentic relationship. Teacher C emphasised the importance of trust: "It is essential to have somebody you can trust. It is the principal." Teacher D further explained this as having to trust the principal to make the right professional decisions as "sometimes you won't get yes ... but you need to trust whatever he says. He has the experience of years, and you know if he's saying no for something there will be a valid reason." Ten of the 12 teachers identified that, to trust the principal, they had to rely on the principal to support them when dealing with challenging situations. Though trust was seen as being important to the teachers in the study, other research has noted that, for trust to develop, it must be founded on authenticity (Branson & Marra, 2019).

The data from the research clearly identified that authentic leadership is more than a skills approach; it is about leaders developing authentic relationships with their teachers and these relationships that are characterised by values such as trust (Gardner et al., 2005). By engaging in these relationships, leaders can better understand their teachers' development and growth and then support them in a meaningful and professional manner.

Being present

Though there is limited literature looking specifically at the principal's presence in schools, Giles (2019) does allude to this when discussing the importance of context and that leaders need to be aware of the context and situations they find themselves in, rather than looking to apply theory. Being present and visible around the school creates opportunities for the principal to engage with teachers and to get to know them. These interactions are reciprocal as they also provide an opportunity for teachers to engage with the principal. The data from the study highlighted the importance teachers placed on their principal's visible presence within the school. The importance of having a presence is also acknowledged by the Ministry of Education on their Educational Leaders website.[1]

However, for the teachers in this study, this was not just about the principal being physically within the school; they wanted to see the principal actively engaging with them, the children, and the wider

---

1   https://www.educationalleaders.govt.nz/

school community. Teacher E gave an example of this: "If we're out there on duty, it's good to see that she's out there helping too." Being in classrooms was also appreciated by the teachers and was seen as the principals actively engaging with the teachers and children. As Teacher F said, "He's always out in classrooms and talking to the children about their learning." Visiting classrooms also served a further purpose from the teachers' perspective in that it was about the principal engaging with them and getting to know them, and they were able to build a personal relationship based on these interactions. Teacher G explained by using the example of the principal regularly popping in and asking if they were okay, and how their day was going. For the teachers, these informal social encounters were viewed as the principal taking an interest in them personally. Teacher B emphasised this by saying, "He takes the time to ask about me and this indicates that he wants to know about me as a person." These desired interactions, that are perceived as being important by teachers, cannot happen without the principal being a relational leader and involved socially within the school context (Branson & Marra, 2019).

Informal encounters

The development of a relationship between principals and teachers can occur during both formal and informal social encounters. In the study, teachers emphasised their principals being present in the informal social networks of the school. All 12 teachers interviewed believed it was important for the principal to take part in social events as it gave them an opportunity to get to know the principal on a more personal level. This notion of getting to know the principal is shared by Branson and Marra (2019), who identify the importance of leaders getting to know the people they are leading by means of developing relationships. For example, in Teacher C's view, "social relationships are the most important thing in teaching." If the principal did not attend social events "then that relationship wouldn't be there". These informal encounters also occurred every day; for example, during morning tea or lunch breaks. Such informal encounters created opportunities for the teachers and principals to understand each other based on sharing personal information on their life outside school.

In addition, informal encounters between teachers and principals were professionally enhancing as professional relationships developed. Teacher F explained, "I think having strong informal relationships help you to understand that more personal level. Maybe you need the personal level to strengthen the formal level one." Teacher H added that "people tend to talk more when they're in a relaxed sort of situation where they feel comfortable talking, and funnily enough, you get more [teaching] ideas from each other over the photocopier". These informal interactions with the principal were also considered by the teachers as opportunities to problem solve and gain further ideas for their teaching practice.

Conclusion

This chapter has drawn on the findings from research that looked at the relationships between principals and teachers. What was clear for the teachers was that relationships count and that it is via these relationships that they get to know and understand their principal. It was also evident that these relationships are reciprocal and evolved over time. For teachers in the study, knowing the principal as a person is important not only for making connections but also for seeing the principal as being authentic and a person they can trust.

As has been identified earlier, teaching is a relational activity and this relationship for teachers is not only with the children in their classroom but also with their principal. From the teachers' perspectives, there were some key aspects identified that allowed them to see the principal as their leader and to engage in a more relational connection with them. For principals, this research has highlighted the importance of taking time to develop a relationship with their teachers. Often this requires deliberate actions on behalf of the principal. As principals take up their roles, their focus should not only be on management but also on relationship building and developing a more relational approach to leadership. As Branson and Marra (2019) state, "What establishes the existence of leadership are the relationships" (p. 101). This understanding of a more relational approach to leadership in schools is an area that would benefit from further research. Such research could take a more nuanced look at what helps principals to develop a more relational leadership approach and what the outcomes would be for teachers, and ultimately for students' learning.

References

Avolio, B. J., Gardner, W. L., Walumbwa, F. O., Luthans, F., & May, D. R. (2004). Unlocking the mask: A look at the process by which authentic leaders impact follower attitudes and behaviors. *The Leadership Quarterly, 15*(6), 801–823.

Begley, P. (2006). Prerequisites to authentic leadership. *Journal of Educational Administration, 44*(6), 570–580.

Blumer, H. (1969). *Symbolic interactionism.* Prentice-Hall.

Branson, C. M., Franken, M., & Penney, D. (2016). Middle leadership in higher education: A relational analysis. *Educational Management, Administration & Leadership, 44*(1), 128–145. https://doi.org/10.1177/1741143214558575

Branson, C. M., Marra, M., Franken, M., & Penney, D. (2018). *Leadership in higher education from a transrelational perspective* (1st ed.). Bloomsbury Publishing.

Branson, M., & Marra, M. (2019). Leadership as a relational phenomenon: What this means in practice. *Research in Educational Administration & Leadership, 4*(1), 81–108. https://doi.org/10.30828/real/2019.1.4

Caza, A., & Jackson, B. (2011). Authentic leadership. In A. Bryman, D. Collinson, K. Grint, B. Jackson, & M. Uhl-Bien (Eds.), *The SAGE handbook of leadership* (pp. 352–364). SAGE Publications.

Crevani, L., Lindgren, M., & Packendorff, J. (2010). Leadership, not leaders: On the study of leadership as practices and interactions. *Scandinavian Journal of Management, 26*(1), 77–86. https://doi.org/10.1016/j.scaman.2009.12.003

Daly, A. J. (2010). Acknowledgements. In A. J. Daly (Ed.), *Social network theory and pedagogical change* (pp. ix–x). Harvard Education Press.

Franken, M., Branson, C., and Penney, D. (2018). A theory-to-practice leadership learning arrangement in a university context. *International Journal of Leadership in Education. 21*(4), 491–505. https://doi.org/10.1080/13603124.2016.1247196

Gardner, W. L., Avolio, B. J., Luthans, F., May, D. R., & Walumbwa, F. (2005). "Can you see the real me?" A self-based model of authentic leader and follower development. *The Leadership Quarterly, 16*(3), 343–372. https://doi.org/10.1016/j.leaqua.2005.03.00

Giles, D., Smythe, E., & Spence, D. (2012). Exploring relationships in education: A phenomenological inquiry. *Australian Journal of Adult Learning, 52*(2), 214–236.

Giles, D. L. (2019). *Relational leadership in education: A phenomenon of inquiry and practice.* Routledge.

Haslam, S. A., Reicher, S. D., & Platow, M. J. (2011). *The new psychology of leadership.* Psychology Press.

Maritsa, E., Goula, A., Psychogios, A., & Pierrakos, G. (2022). Leadership development: Exploring relational leadership implications in healthcare organizations. *International Journal of Environmental Research and Public Health, 19*(23), 15971. https://doi.org/10.3390/ijerph192315971

Ministry of Education. (2008). *Kiwi leadership for principals: Principals as educational* leaders.https://www.educationalleaders.govt.nz/Leadership-development/Key-leadership-documents/Kiwi-leadership-for-principals

Timperley, H., Ell, F., Le Fevre, D., & Twyford, K. (2020). *Leading professional learning: Practical strategies for impact in schools.* ACER Press.

Timperley, H., & Hulsbosch, N. (2010). *Instructional leadership in action.* [Paper presentation]. Change through Conversations: Instructional Leadership in Action symposium, American Educational Research Association, Denver.

Wheatley, M. (2006). *Leadership and new science: Discovering order in a chaotic world* (3rd ed.). Berrett-Koehler.

INDEX

achievement for underperforming groups 115
Action Plan for Pacific Education 2020–2030 (Ministry of Education, 2020) 24, 29
administrative role of leaders 117–18, 123–24, 146, 149, 158–59
aki (akiaki) 10
ako 107–08
ariki 4, 5
aroha 11, 15
"Aspiring Leaders" programme 94
assimilation 6, 8
associate teacher leadership during practicum 101–02, 104, 108–09
    ako 105–08
    communication 102–03, 106
    mentoring 103–05, 107, 108
    relationships 101–02, 104
    vulnerability 106–08
authentic leadership 161
biculturalism 8, 154
bilingual education 8
caring of others 65–66
change initiatives *see* educational change
Christianity 28
churches in Pacific communities 26, 28
collaboration
    collaborative culture 36–38, 39
    in early childhood leadership 63, 64, 66, 69, 81, 88
    by middle leaders 147, 149, 150, 153, 154
    in primary schools 122–23, 128, 135, 138–39, 160
    see also cross-sector collaboration
collectivism 6, 7, 9, 27, 61, 64
collegial support 36–38, 39, 64, 65, 66, 67–68, 78, 134, 135
colonisation 6, 8
communication 4, 10, 23, 66–67, 79–80, 88–89, 101, 136, 149, 153
    by associate teachers during practicum 102–03, 104
communities of practice 88, 89, 93, 97
community–school relationships
    during COVID-19 pandemic 79–80, 82, 126
    in early childhood education 89
    Kāhui Ako | Communities of Learning 35–36
    Māori communities 127
    Pacific communities 25, 127
    Pacific peoples 25, 26–27
    in primary education 126–28
complex problems 44–45
compliance with regulations 123–24
confidence 24, 29, 51, 56, 93, 94, 95, 104, 106, 107, 137, 150, 153
COVID-19 pandemic experience of ECE leaders 72–73, 82, 120, 125, 126
    approaches to teaching and learning 80
    communication 79–80, 126
    description of the study 73–74
    impact on leaders' wellbeing 74–75, 120
    lack of support to manage and solve problems 77
    staffing issues 77–78
    strategies for effective leadership 78–83
    support networks 79
    volume of evolving information 75–76
critical friendship 68
cross-sector collaboration 32–34, 35–38, 39
    as a professional opportunity 41
    see also Kāhui Ako | Communities of Learning; systems-convening leadership
culture 10
    norms 23
    of Pacific peoples 21, 22, 23, 24–25, 27–29
curriculum 6, 8, 12, 24–25, 39, 52, 80, 93, 95, 120, 150, 151, 152–53, 154
    see also New Zealand Curriculum; Te Whāriki

decolonisation 8
deep learning 51
delegation 80–82
digital technology 125, 126
dispositional leadership approach 61–62, 64–70
distance teaching 78
distributed leadership 63, 64, 67, 74, 80–82, 94, 102, 151

early childhood (ECE) leadership 61–62, 69–70, 102, 109
    changing perception of ECE leadership 63–64
    critical aspects of effective leadership 88–91
    dispositional approach 64–69
    hindrances 62–63, 69
    need for training 62–63, 67–68
    opportunities for implementing leadership 95–96
    postgraduate leadership programme study 87–88, 96–97
postgraduate leadership programme study, impacts on participants 91–97
    see also COVID-19 pandemic experience of ECE leaders
early childhood education (ECE) 85
    see also under educational change
ECE Taskforce (2011) 62
Educa 80
Education Act 1967 6
Education Review Office 116
educational change 46–48, 62, 132
    in early childhood education 63–64, 68–69, 85, 92, 93–94
    emotional responses 44–47, 56
    framework for navigating emotional responses 49–55
    influence of past and current experiences 48
    knowledge and credibility of leaders 52
    knowledge and understanding of the process 50–52
    resistance by teachers 47–48, 48
    see also primary teacher change and transition
Educational Leadership Capability Framework (ELCF) (Education Council, 2018) 86, 92–93, 116
Educational Leadership Model (ELM) 118
emergent and potential leadership 62, 63, 64, 65, 67–69, 70, 81, 92, 94, 121–23, 151
emotional intelligence 104
emotions 43–49, 51, 53, 56, 79, 101, 136, 137
empathy 9, 22, 54, 58, 88, 89–90, 104
Employee Assistance Program (EAP) 82
empowerment 8, 10, 50, 67, 68–69, 80–82, 93, 95, 104, 107
English language 6, 23
"essential workers" during COVID-19 pandemic 78
ethnicity challenge for Pacific leadership 22–23

Falalalaga (Samoan) model 25
Fale Hanga (Tongan) model 25
family–school relationships *see* community–school relationships
feedback 66
fono (meetings) 26
funding 85, 123, 124–25, 154

gender challenge for Pacific leadership 22–23

hapū 4, 5, 6, 9
health and safety compliance 123
hierarchical leadership 61, 62, 63 69, 122–23

identity 10, 87
    Māori 6, 7, 8
    Pacific peoples 24, 25, 28
    professional identity 46, 53, 95–96, 108, 140

inclusion 10, 90, 107, 116, 148, 154
individualism 6, 9
intergenerational learning 5, 11
iwi 4–5, 6, 9

Kāhui Ako | Communities of Learning 32, 33, 40–41, 116, 129
    collaborative culture and collegial support 36–38, 39
    description of the study 34–35
    diverse teacher expertise 38–40
    see also cross-sector collaboration; systems-convening leadership
kaikaranga 7
karakia 11
karanga 7
kaumātua 4, 7, 8
kaupapa Māori concepts 87
knowledge
    of effective leaders 52, 90–91, 93, 94, 95–96
    tension between roles of CEO and leader of school learning 118–19
    transmission and acquisition 105–06
Kōhanga Reo 8
kotahitanga (unity and oneness) 7
kuia 7
kura kaupapa Māori (Māori immersion schooling) 8

language 10
    barriers for Pacific teachers 23
    official languages of New Zealand 11
    Pacific languages 24, 25, 29
    see also English language; te reo Māori
leadership 101–02
    critical aspects of effective leadership 88–91
    development of capability 62, 63, 64, 65, 67–69, 70, 81, 92, 94, 121–23, 151
    effective leadership 86–87
    leadership style 102, 158–59, 160–62
    research and guidance 115–17
    see also associate teacher leadership during practicum; early childhood (ECE) leadership; Māori leadership; middle leadership; Pacific leadership; relational leadership; "school leadership"; systems-convening leadership

Learning in a Covid-19 World (Education Review Office, 2021) 74, 76, 79

mana 10
mana motuhake (self-determination) 7
manaaki 11
manaakitanga 4, 10, 14
manawhenua 26
manuheri (guests) 9, 10
Māori communities 127
Māori leadership 3–4, 87
    framework 8–12
    historical context: broken harmony 6
    historical context: harmony 4–5
    historical context: rebuilding of harmony 7–8
    types of leaders 5
    whakapapa 4
Māori society
    cultural values 4, 6, 7, 8
    social structures 4, 6
Māori teachers in mission schools 6
marae 4, 5, 9, 26
    manaakitanga 10
mātauranga Māori principles 8–15, 16
    see also the individual principles, e.g. whakapapa
mauri ora 11, 15
mentoring 67, 92, 103–05, 107, 108, 122, 137
middle leadership 146–48
    characteristics of middle leaders 150–51, 153
    definitions 146–47
    practices 150, 153
    in primary schools 145–46, 150–55
    roles 147–48
    saying, doing and relating 147, 148
    support for middle leaders 154
    vignette of a middle leader 151–54
Middle Leadership in Schools (MLiS) model 148–50
Ministry of Education 116, 118, 123, 124, 125, 165
mission schools 6

motivation 29, 40, 63, 64, 67, 69, 102, 104, 151, 161

National Education Learning Priorities (NELP) (Ministry of Education, 2020) 116, 119
Native Schools Act 6
neurodiverse learners 125
New Zealand Curriculum (Ministry of Education, 2007) 9

organisational role of middle leaders 149
Our Schooling Futures: Stronger Together (Tomorrow's Schools Independent Taskforce, 2018) 115–16

Pacific leadership 20, 29–30, 87
challenges 22–23
chiefs' authority 20, 21
connections with Māori and other communities 26
difficulty in progressing to decision-making levels 23
framework 23–24
history 20–21
key principles 24–28
practising attributes 26–27, 28–29
presence within communities 26–27
as role models 22
strengths brought to leadership roles 22
support networks 29
training programmes 29
underrepresentation in ECE and schools 21–22, 29
Pacific peoples
Aotearoa New Zealand population 21
community relationships 25, 127
integrating communities into schools and ECE centres 26–27
values 27–29
Papatūānuku (mother earth) 4
paperwork 118, 123
parent–teacher meetings 27
Pasifika festival 24
pepeha 9

personal attributes of effective leaders 89–90
practicum experience 99–100, 108–09
ako 105–06
communication 102–04, 104
mentoring 103–05, 107, 108
relationship building 101–02, 104
vulnerablity 106–08
primary school leadership 115–17, 128–29, 132–33
challenges 123–29
description of the study of role and challenges 117
developing capability 121–23
how leaders see their role 118
inequities in resourcing, funding and salaries 124–25
middle leadership 145–46, 150–55
pace and cost of compliance 122–24
societal shifts and changing expectations 125–27
support of staff 132–33, 134–39, 141, 154, 161–62
tension between CEO and leader of learning roles 118–19, 128
wellbeing and relational trust 119–21
see also relational leadership
primary teacher change and transition 132–33, 140–41
common vision 139–40
description of the study 133
professional learning opportunities 132, 133, 134, 141
role of school leaders 132–33, 134–39, 141
support for teachers 136–38
professional learning 44, 46, 48, 49, 51, 51
in early childhood leadership 62–63, 67, 69, 85–86
for middle leaders 150
in primary teacher change process 132, 133, 134, 141
pūrākau (storytelling) 9, 11

rangatira 4, 5
Ranginui (sky father) 4

reciprocity 27, 65, 66
reflection 89, 96, 104
relational leadership 158–59, 167–68
description of the study 159–60
informal encounters between principals and teachers 162–63, 166–67
principal's presence and interaction in schools 165–66
styles 160–62
teachers' perspectives on building relationships with principals 162–67
relational trust 36–38, 39, 43, 53, 56, 65, 67, 119–21, 135–36, 164–65
relationships 10, 22
central role in education 158
learning-focused relationships 54
during the practicum experience 101–02, 104
productive working relationships 68
relationship-focused leadership 61, 65
see also community–school relationships; *vā* (sacred relationships between people)
reporting requirements 124
resourcing 124–25
respect 8, 9, 10, 13, 14, 27, 54, 56, 65, 66, 67, 104, 127
responsiveness 65, 66
risk 43
perceptions of risk 47–48, 49, 53, 56
risk-taking 46
supportive risk-taking 49, 50, 53, 54–55, 56
role models 22, 62, 81, 86, 102, 107, 121
Royal Society Te Apārangi 152

salaries 124–25
"school leadership" 115
research and guidance 115–17
School Leadership and Student Outcomes (Robinson et al., 2009) 115
science teaching leadership programme 152, 153
self-managing schools 118, 145
self-reflection 89, 96
skills for leadership 88–89

social media 125, 126
societal shifts and changing expectations 125–27
special needs children 125
spirituality
Pacific peoples 21, 28
see also wairua (spirituality)
staff development role of middle leaders 149
staffing 85, 124–25
COVID-19 issues 76, 77, 78–79
Storypark 80
strategic role of middle leaders 149
strategic thinking and leadership 93
student-focused role of middle leaders 149
supervisory role of middle leaders 149
systems-convening leadership 32–34, 38, 40–41
collaborative culture built on relational trust 36–38
communicating a clear vision for improvement 35–36
see also cross-sector collaboration; Kāhui Ako | Communities of Learning

talanoa (free-flowing conversation between people) 22
tangata whenua 10
tangata whenuatanga 12
Tapasā (Ministry of Education, 2018) 24, 25–26
Tātaiako: Cultural Competencies for Teachers of Māori Learners (Education Council New Zealand, 2011) 12

Tauhivā ako 106
te ao Māori 4–5, 9, 105
Te Atairangikaahu, Te Arikinui Dame 5
Te Māori exhibition, 1986 7
te reo Māori 5, 11
erosion 6
rights 7
te reo me ōna tikanga Māori 8, 9, 11, 14
Te Tiriti o Waitangi 6, 7, 8
Te Whāriki (Ministry of Education, 1996, 2017) 9, 24

teacher-leaders 61–62
teachers
connection with families and children during COVID-19 pandemic 79–80, 126
diverse teacher expertise 38–40
knowledge and credibility 52, 68
leadership development 62, 63, 64, 65, 67–69, 70, 81, 92, 95, 121–23, 151
perspectives on building relationships with principals 162–67
professional efficacy 63
resistance to change initiatives 46–47, 48
see also associate teacher leadership during practicum; primary teacher change and transition
Teaching Council of Aotearoa New Zealand 61, 62, 68, 69
team environment 64, 65–69, 90, 92, 93, 154
tohunga 4, 5
Tomorrow's Schools Independent Taskforce 115–16, 124
Tomorrow's Schools policy 118, 145
trans-relational leadership 161–62
trust 102, 104
developing cultures of trust 49, 53, 54, 81
relational trust 36–38, 39, 43, 53, 56, 65, 67, 118–21, 135–36, 164–65
Tū Rangatira–Māori Medium Educational Leadership (Ministry of Education, 2010) 115

uncertainty 43, 47, 48, 50, 55, 73, 78, 79

vā (sacred relationships between people) 27–28
vaccine mandates, COVID-19 pandemic 77
vulnerability 44, 46, 47, 48, 49, 50, 51, 53, 56
during the practicum 106–08

waiata 5, 9, 11
wairua (spirituality) 11
wānanga 5
wellbeing 74–75, 79, 82, 90, 103, 113–14, 119–21
whakakoakoa (happiness, joy) 11
whakapapa 4

mātauranga Māori principle 9–10, 13
practices of saying whakapapa 5, 9
variation 9
whakapono (belief, trust) 11
Whakaputanga o te Rangatiratanga o Nu Tireni (Declaration of the Independence of New Zealand) 6, 7
whakataukī 5, 6, 9, 11
whānau 4, 5, 6
on the marae 9
participation 8, 10
whanaungatanga 4
mātauranga Māori principle 10, 13
working from home 78, 80
workload 74, 80, 117, 118, 136

Zoom calls and meetings 73, 79, 80

ABOUT THE AUTHORS

Monica Cameron (EdD) has been involved in early childhood education as a student, teacher, professional development facilitator and lecturer for more than 25 years. She has been working in Initial Teacher Education since 2011 and is currently a senior lecturer at Te Rito Maioha. Her teaching and research interests include early childhood assessment, curriculum, pedagogy, leadership, evaluation, inclusion, and critical reflection. Monica is committed to supporting pre-service and in-service teachers to further their learning through study and research, while continuing to be a learner herself.

Tracey Carlyon (PhD) is the Research Leader at Te Rito Maioha and an adjunct professor at UNITAR International University. She has been involved in education for over 25 years and has experience teaching at all levels of the curriculum. Her roles have included primary school teacher and leader; senior lecturer in initial teacher education at Waikato University; and teaching and learning coach at Wintec. Both Tracey's master's and doctoral studies focused on transitions, the place of leadership, and how transitions can provide opportunities for professional learning. She has a particular interest and passion for coaching and mentoring.

Gwen Davitt (MEd) is an active researcher, professional development facilitator and educator with an extensive background in adult teaching and learning, leadership, and early childhood education. In her career, Gwen has been involved in multiple programmes from diploma to post-graduate level. Current research interests include knowledge, skills and dispositions of leadership, social and emotional competence, and an exploration of the nuances and challenges of the home-based education and care sector. As a lifelong learner, Gwen is passionate about integrating theory and practice, reflective practice, the pedagogies of teaching and learning, navigating leadership, and leading change for best practice.

Richard Edwards (MSc) is a senior lecturer at Te Rito Maioha. He has been involved in supporting teacher professional learning, both in-service, and pre-service, for over 30 years. He has taught in a range of teacher education programmes in New Zealand and overseas. His research interests include curriculum, assessment, and professional learning particularly in the areas of science education, technology education, and sustainability education. He is currently involved in research in STEM education in primary schools.

Jo Ellis (MEd) has a career in education which spans more than 42 years and includes the roles of teacher, head teacher, professional development facilitator, licensing officer for Ministry of Education, lecturer, director of five ECE centres and three home-based centres in Dunedin. Jo completed her Master of Education in 2006, based on Women Reflecting on Learning. Most recently she was the assistant principal at Qatar Academy in Qatar. She joined Te Rito Maioha in 2021 as the Regional Education Leader and lecturer in Ōtepoti.

Anthony Fisher (MA) is the Academic Leader Primary Programmes at Te Rito Maioha. He has experience teaching at all levels of the curriculum. His roles have included primary school teacher and principal; educational psychologist, leader/manager at regional and national levels for special education, and senior lecturer in initial teacher education at Waikato University. Anthony's research interests have focused on the areas of transition within the teaching profession, teachers moving across levels and into senior leadership positions, and the relational aspects of leadership. Also, he has a particular interest in coaching and mentoring for beginning teachers.

Beth Germaine (MEdLship) is the Programme Leader for the Graduate Diploma of Teaching (Primary) at Te Rito Maioha, bringing over 25 years of experience teaching and leading professional learning within the primary sector in Aotearoa New Zealand. Her leadership is driven by a deep commitment to enhancing educational outcomes for ākonga, achieved through supporting teachers in refining their pedagogical practices. Beth has a particular focus on curriculum design and implementation, with extensive expertise in mathematics, social sciences, and integrated and conceptual curricula. Currently, she is engaged in research on principal leadership in curriculum development in primary schools.

Anoop Kumar (EdD) is a senior lecturer in primary education at Te Rito Maioha. Anoop has been involved in teacher education in New Zealand and in Fiji for over 25 years. His research interests include education for minorities and marginalised learners. His doctoral study focused on teachers' experiences with refugee children and their families in New Zealand. Anoop is committed to supporting quality teacher education programmes.

Clark McPhillips (MEd) is the Primary Sector Engagement Leader at Te Rito Maioha. With over 20 years' experience in primary school education, ranging from classroom teaching to principal, he has dedicated the past decade to initial teacher education. Clark has expertise in practicum, field-based experiences, and mentoring aspiring educators. He is deeply committed to fostering educational excellence and innovation within primary education. In his role, he advocates for a practical, hands-on approach and emphasises the significance of real-world experience. He is dedicated to cultivating strong partnerships between educational institutions and schools, aiming to enhance the quality of teacher preparation.

Debbie Ryder (PhD) is the Master of Education Programme Leader for Te Rito Maioha and is a senior lecturer and thesis supervisor. Debbie has worked in education for over 30 years and has taught in ECE, initial teacher education and master's level. Her work includes researching teacher registration at master's level, and contradictions in physical activity in her doctoral studies. More recently Appreciative Inquiry has been a keen area of research interest. Leadership has been a key focus in PLD that Debbie has facilitated alongside a previous colleague. More recently Debbie is working with other colleagues in relational leadership.

Penny Smith (PhD) has been active in the early childhood sector for almost 40 years. She has taught in kindergartens, holding both teacher and head teacher positions. Penny now works in the tertiary sector and is a senior lecturer and Academic Leader of the Postgraduate Programmes at Te Rito Maioha. She is a lifelong learner whose research interests include peer learning, leadership and early childhood curriculum. Penny's doctoral research was a mixed methods investigation about teacher's knowledge, beliefs and practices related to peer learning. She has a strong interest in governance and has held leadership roles on governance boards.

Tui Summers (EdD) is dedicated to the early childhood education profession. Her professional experience has included ECE teaching, lecturing in initial teacher education, policy, education evaluation and leadership roles. She has completed master's study on inclusive education and doctoral study focused on indigenous leadership. Tui has a depth and breadth of expertise focused on early childhood education, initial teacher education, quality assurance, leadership, kaupapa Māori and mātauranga Māori. She has a strong commitment to and is passionate about Te Tiriti o Waitangi, social justice, and equity for all learners.

Rachel Taylor (MEd) has 18 years' experience as an early childhood teacher out of which she has spent 10 years working with infants and toddlers. She feels passionate about Te Rito Maioha's bicultural commitment which inspired her to take the role of kaiako after completing her study. Rachel recently completed her Master of Education which was based on parents' experiences in early childhood education sector during the COVID-19 pandemic in 2022.

Sandra Tuhakaraina (MEd) (Ngāti Kahungunu ki Wairoa) is a teacher educator for Te Rito Maioha. She is a senior lecturer/pouako matua, course leader/kaiārahi marautanga for the Bachelor of Teaching (ECE) programmes and facilitator in the master's. Before this position, Sandra was a parent, kaiako in Te Kohanga Reo language nest. Sandra's current interest is kaupapa Māori, te reo Māori language learning, and te ao Māori concepts.

Tiffany Williams (MEd) has worked in education since 2009, having completed the early years degree with Massey University. She has actively nurtured an interest in education across different sectors through work in early childhood education, primary, and tertiary sectors. Through Kāhui Ako work and postgraduate study, Tiffany learned about teaching and educational leadership in a wide range of contexts. Her interest led to the completion of her master's degree in 2023 which explored supporting factors of cross-sector collaboration. Tiffany currently works at Te Rito Maioha as a lecturer in the Bachelor of Teaching (ECE) degree.

Claire Wilson (MEd) is a senior lecturer at Te Rito Maioha, working currently in both the Postgraduate Leadership Programme and the Graduate Diploma (ECE) Programme. Claire has over 18 years of experience in both the early childhood education and primary sectors. Claire completed her Master of Education with Massey University, Manawatū; the quality and significance of her research led to her being the joint recipient of the NZARE 2017 Rae Munro Award. Claire brings a strong and realistic vision and commitment for growing both teachers' and leaders' resiliency, and social/educational justice and advocation within the education sector.

Debbie Woolston (MEd) has worked in the kindergarten sector in both teacher and head teacher positions in Auckland and Northland for nearly 30 years and is currently a senior lecturer at Te Rito Maioha in Whangārei. Debbie completed her Master of Education in 2017 based on Associate Teachers in Early Childhood Education—Why early childhood educators choose to be associate teachers and what they perceive is their role. She is passionate about the practicum experience for tauira and working alongside associate teachers to promote leadership within this space.

www.ingramcontent.com/pod-product-compliance
Lightning Source LLC
Chambersburg PA
CBHW061753290426
44108CB00029B/2981